Dangerous Liaisons: *the film*

Dangerous Liaisons: *the film*

A screenplay by CHRISTOPHER HAMPTON

Based on the novel by

PIERRE-AMBROISE-FRANÇOIS CHODERLOS DE LACLOS

faber and faber
LONDON·BOSTON

First published in 1989
by Faber and Faber Limited
3 Queen Square London WCIN 3AU

Printed in Great Britain by
Richard Clay Ltd, Bungay, Suffolk
All rights reserved

A CIP record for this book is available from the British Library.

ISBN 0-571-15447-6

For Stephen Frears

Introduction *My Dinner with Miloš*

What follows is a brief account of how my play *Les Liaisons Dangereuses*, which opened at The Other Place (now sadly defunct) in Stratford in September 1985 for a scheduled twenty-three performances, eventually (and somewhat miraculously) led on to the Warner Brothers' film *Dangerous Liaisons*, which opened in America in December 1988. It was a far from straightforward journey, with more than its fair share of diversions, blind alleys and reckless driving, during which a little of Laclos's military training might have often come in handy: I shall try to confine myself to the principal landmarks.

I sold the film rights to my first play in 1967; since when the bidding for film rights to my work has hardly been brisk. However, in this case, offers for the rights had begun to arrive even before the Royal Shakespeare Company brought the play in to The Pit in January 1986, and in the course of the year, despite the RSC's absent-minded dropping of the play from its schedule for three months, the bids proliferated. I was busy with other things. Still, there seemed to be plenty of time and I thought it was simply a matter of weighing up the various options and making a careful choice. As it turned out, this naïve way of thinking contained a number of important errors.

Not that the film rights could have been sold before the disposition of the New York rights. A management putting an English play on (or off) Broadway traditionally shares with the London management 40 per cent of any film or TV sales; and the cost of mounting a play in New York is now so alarming that the absence of these ancillary rights rules out any possibility of a production. There's a corollary to this: any proposal for a film which seeks to keep costs down by suggesting profit participation rather than a large upfront payment (and there were one or two interesting approaches along these lines) is unlikely to be approved of by the theatre managers or their investors.

In fact, the New York rights had been disposed of, without

my knowledge, before the play had even opened. The RSC has an arrangement with an American producer, James Nederlander, whereby, in return for a certain amount of money, he has first option on any new play the RSC presents. As it turned out, Mr Nederlander had a genuine love for the play and proved more than reasonable, allowing for example the director, Howard Davies, and myself to persuade him, against what I suspect was his commercial instinct, to bring over the British company, rather than recasting with American actors: all the same, the arrangement itself is hardly one of which an author could be expected to approve. And one of its consequences was to put any decision about the film on ice until the Broadway opening in April 1987.

The play's first preview at the Music Box Theatre on 45th St was a more than usually ghastly occasion. During the day the temperature rose steeply and in the course of the afternoon it was discovered that the delicate amplification necessary in so large a house had not been balanced against the air-conditioning, which effectively drowned it. A dispute between the rival claims of art and comfort was decided in favour of the former more or less as the audience filed in. Within a few days, the cast had adjusted to the dimensions of the theatre and were giving as good an account of the play as it had ever received: but there simply had not been enough time to prepare, and on this occasion the performance was muted and tentative. Nevertheless, alongside the representatives from the major studios and other perspiring celebrities, the three chief executives from the Lorimar film division, Bernie Brillstein, Peter Chernin and Ileen Maisel, decided they wanted to acquire the film rights.

Peter and Ileen came to see me the following day. Ileen had been told about the play by Norma Heyman, the English producer for whom I had written a film based on *The Honorary Consul*. The film hadn't turned out quite as we'd hoped, for a variety of reasons, but I'd been very impressed with Norma's commitment, tenacity and attention to detail. One of Lorimar's proposals was that I should co-produce the film (with Norma); obviously, in addition to working with someone I knew well, this would give me the advantage of having some say in the choice of director, cast and so on. Just as important, however, was the fact that I immediately liked Ileen and Peter (and, when I subsequently met him, Bernie) and felt they were to be trusted. I came back to England, deciding to follow my instinct and relieved that the much-deferred disposal of the film rights could finally be made.

Easier said than done. Lorimar, I was assured, was not offering enough money. Furthermore, the company was on the brink of bankruptcy. Various incomprehensible articles to this effect in the trade papers began to arrive weekly in my mail. Most seriously of all, the RSC refused to agree to countersign my contract.

Reading contracts is not one of my skills and I had failed to notice that the RSC had reserved this unlikely right of veto. It was also my understanding that they had handed over 90 per cent of their participation in the film rights to Frank and Woji Gero as part of the West End transfer negotiations. They were therefore entitled to 2 per cent of the film rights. This meant that for them to achieve an extra thousand pounds the basic offer would need to increase by the best part of a hundred thousand dollars. Nevertheless they were adamant. Complete stalemate ensued.

Adjacent or sideways to this was the matter of Miloš Forman. He had been sighted early on in the run of the play at the Pit, more than once by all accounts. He was pointed out to me at the première in New York. Now, a friend of Mr Nederlander's, Salah Hassanein, at this time head of distribution for United Artists, declared an interest in acquiring the rights for Mr Forman, with whom he had attended a screening of Roger Vadim's 1959 film *Les Liaisons Dangereuses* in New York. Would I go with him to meet Mr Forman in Paris? Unfortunately, I was very busy and couldn't get away. In that case, could we all meet the following weekend in London? Of course.

Mr Hassanein and I arrived at Mr Forman's hotel at the appointed hour on Saturday 30 May. He had not checked in. We waited a while, then moved on to a restaurant, where we enjoyed an excellent meal. We reminisced about a school we had both attended in Alexandria. The atmosphere was convivial. Mr Forman, however, failed to join us. I went home.

The stalemate persisted through the summer. I went on holiday with my family to Crete. There, I was telephoned by my agent, who told me that Miloš Forman had announced his intention to make a film based on *Les Liaisons Dangereuses*. It would be called *Valmont* and it would have nothing to do with my play. The good news was that the R S C had been sufficiently galvanized by this information to countersign the contract with Lorimar. Too late, I said. I was convinced that in these circumstances no one would ever go ahead with our film.

I returned to New York in September in a melancholy frame of mind. The British cast had completed its Equity-permitted twenty weeks on Broadway and the play closed, breaking the theatre's house record in its final week. The air was thick with valediction. However, Lorimar seemed as optimistic as ever. They were still talking to Miloš Forman's agents and lawyers (the man himself being notably hard to come by); indeed they were talking to all kinds of people. I should go back to England and stand by.

A month passed; then, in the manner of films, forced inactivity was suddenly transformed into frantic haste. Mr Forman was sitting with his writer in Connecticut, beavering away. We were now months behind. Unless we caught up with, not to say overtook the opposition, all was lost.

The first draft was written in less than a month and delivered on Thanksgiving weekend, 1987. It was enthusiastically received, but my sense is that the following three weeks or so were the most perilous of the entire saga. Fortunately, I know no details of what went on and all that can be said in retrospect is that Bernie Brillstein managed to overcome whatever doubts and difficulties remained; at last, the questions of director and cast, the subject of endless theoretical discussions, could be addressed in some concrete way.

Lorimar had one instinct in common with all the other companies who had negotiated for the rights: a disinclination to cast anyone connected with the play. They didn't ask for big stars; they didn't even demand American actors; they simply wanted a fresh start. I often wondered whether their decision had anything to do with the circumstances of that first preview in New York; they denied this and insisted, however hard I argued, that what they felt was necessary was a cast who would arrive on the set not carrying any kind of baggage.

An actor whose name began to surface frequently in our discussions was John Malkovich; so, in the week before Christmas, I went back to New York and saw the play in which he was appearing, Lanford Wilson's *Burn This*. The performance was an astonishing *tour de force*. Afterwards, I went backstage, knocked on his dressing-room door, introduced myself and handed him the script. His immediate acceptance of the part of Valmont felt like a great breakthrough: finally, we were up and running.

At the same time I persuaded Lorimar to let me show the script to Stephen Frears. Such reluctance as they had displayed was entirely to do with the fact that he had never before made a large-budget film. It's always seemed to me more logical to be wary of a man who has never made a small-budget film, but there we are. Anyway, back in London, I went round to hand him the script on New Year's Day 1988.

He seemed to like it. And so, a few weeks later, it was back to New York for Stephen to meet Bernie Brillstein. The atmosphere at lunch was initially somewhat strained and Stephen, who to mark the solemnity of the occasion had invested in a new pair of sneakers, was asked how soon he was able to begin work. After an impressive pause for reflection, he said, 'Tuesday'. He then proposed a five-week trial period, during which he and I could work on the script, while he investigated the feasibility of the budget and timetable and began to assemble a team. As to the casting, he was more than happy with John Malkovich and before his stay in New York was over and a delighted Lorimar could realistically contemplate the prospect of beginning shooting in a little over three months, he had agreed to offer the part of the Marquise de Merteuil to Glenn Close.

I had met Glenn the year before with Howard Davies, when we had asked her to head the American company we had expected to take over the play on Broadway when the RSC's permitted time was up. She had accepted and had then, no doubt, been as startled as we were when the management decided not to extend the run. Apart from any other considerations, it therefore seemed only just that the part should eventually come to her.

The next three months sped by in a blur. Exhaustive script discussions took place (mostly in aeroplanes) and I wrote two more drafts; the enormous apparatus of pre-production trundled forward; location hunts established, to general relief, that it was scarcely more expensive to shoot in France than in Eastern Europe or elsewhere; rehearsals took place at Glenn's house in the country (she was about to have a baby). A good deal of time was devoted to the casting of Madame de Tourvel and Stephen and I met some impressive candidates both in New York and Los Angeles. We decided to offer the part to Michelle Pfeiffer. A mysterious silence ensued. Subsequently it turned out that she had simultaneously been offered the part of Madame de Merteuil in Miloš Forman's film. For a week, as everyone at our end hyperventilated, she had been driving to work (she was shooting *Tequila Sunrise*) with both scripts on the seat beside her. Eventually, to our great good fortune, she made her choice.

At last, we were standing, soon after dawn, inadequately protected from the drizzle, outside Château Maisons-Lafitte, a grandiose pile playing the part of Madame de Rosemonde's country house. There were still a good many surprises in store, not the least of which was that in that first week of shooting, the film was bought lock, stock and barrel by Warner Bros. in a deal separate from their interminable negotiations to buy Lorimar. We were to suffer none of the interference often associated with big studios and they proved exemplary custodians of the film: which now began, as John Malkovich paused at the top of a flight of stone steps, silhouetted against a leaden sky, and slapped his boot with his glove. It was 30 May: a year to the day since I'd failed to have dinner with Miloš Forman.

Published screenplays often consist of the writer's final draft or shooting script. The inevitable differences between such a text and the finished film can be fascinating, but seem sometimes to imply a kind of reproach or criticism. In this case, since the film was a genuinely collaborative venture, I wanted the screenplay to resemble the final cut as closely as possible. It follows that I owe thanks to all those who contributed to the final shape of the film, principally, of course, Stephen Frears, but also the actors, the editing room, the camera team, designers, continuity, the sound department, fellow producers, executives, preview audiences in Pasadena and just about anybody who put a head round the door and lobbed in a suggestion. I'm extremely grateful.

Christopher Hampton

Warner Bros. presents a Lorimar Film Entertainment picture
of an NFH Limited Production:

DANGEROUS LIAISONS

starring

Glenn Close   John Malkovich   Michelle Pfeiffer
Swoosie Kurtz   Keanu Reeves   Mildred Natwick
Uma Thurman

Director Stephen Frears
Screenplay Christopher Hampton
Producers Norma Heyman *and* Hank Moonjean
Based on the play by Christopher Hampton
Adapted from the novel Les Liaisons Dangereuses by Choderlos
   de Laclos
Director of Photography Philippe Rousselot
Production Designer Stuart Craig
Film Editor Mick Audsley
Co-Producer Christopher Hampton
Music George Fenton
Costume Designer James Acheson
Production Supervisor Suzanne Wiesenfeld
Casting Juliet Taylor *and* Howard Feuer

CAST

MARQUISE DE MERTEUIL	Glenn Close
VICOMTE DE VALMONT	John Malkovich
MADAME DE TOURVEL	Michelle Pfeiffer
MADAME DE VOLANGES	Swoosie Kurtz
CHEVALIER DANCENY	Keanu Reeves
MADAME DE ROSEMONDE	Mildred Natwick
CÉCILE DE VOLANGES	Uma Thurman
AZOLAN	Peter Capaldi
GEORGES	Joe Sheridan
JULIE	Valerie Gogan
ÉMILIE	Laura Benson
ADELE	Joanna Pavlis
MAJORDOMO	Nicholas Hawtrey
CASTRATO	Paulo Abel Do Nascimento
CURÉ	François Lalande
BELLEROCHE	François Montagut
ARMAND	Harry Jones
BAILIFF	Christian Erickson
OPERA SINGER	Catherine Cauwet

Produced on the Broadway Stage by
James M. Nederlander,
The Shubert Organization Inc., Jerome Minskoff,
Elizabeth I. McCann and Stephen Graham in
association with Jonathan Farkas

Original Royal Shakespeare Company Production presented
in the West End of London by Frank and Woji Gero

Original Stage Production
in Stratford-upon-Avon, London and New York
by the
Royal Shakespeare Company

INT. MERTEUIL'S DRESSING-ROOM. DAY
The gilt frame around the mirror on the MARQUISE DE
MERTEUIL'*s dressing-table encloses the reflection of her beautiful
face. For a moment she examines herself; critically, but not
without satisfaction.
Another angle shows the whole large room, the early afternoon
light filtering through gauze curtains.
It's midsummer in Paris in 1788.*

INT. VICOMTE DE VALMONT'S BEDROOM. DAY
VALMONT *is an indistinct shape in his vast bed. His valet-de-
chambre,* AZOLAN, *leads a troupe of male servants into the room.
One raises the blind and opens enough of a curtain to admit some
afternoon light; another waits with a cup of chocolate steaming on
a tray; a third carries a damp flannel in a bowl; another pours
water into a bathtub.* VALMONT *stirs, his face still unseen, and
reaches for the flannel.*

INT. MERTEUIL'S DRESSING-ROOM. DAY
*Three or four female servants wait, disposed around the room, as
Merteuil's chambermaid leans over* MERTEUIL, *polishing her
shoulders with crushed mother-of-pearl.*

INT. VALMONT'S BEDROOM. DAY
VALMONT'*s face is swathed in hot towels, his head tilted back. A
young manicurist, on his knees, attends to* VALMONT'*s nails.
Several other servants wait gravely to play their part in the
elaborate ritual of dressing* VALMONT. *The barber produces a
pair of tweezers and delicately plucks a hair from one of*
VALMONT'*s nostrils.*

INT. MERTEUIL'S DRESSING-ROOM. DAY
Merteuil's maid straps a pair of bamboo panniers on to
MERTEUIL'*s waist.*

I

INT. VALMONT'S BEDROOM. DAY
AZOLAN *opens a walk-in closet, which contains innumerable rows
of boots and shoes. He and another servant choose a couple of
pairs of shoes each and bring them out.* VALMONT*'s hand comes
into shot, indicating a black pair with red heels.* AZOLAN *hands
them to a bootboy, who hurries away, breathing on them as he
goes.*

INT. MERTEUIL'S DRESSING-ROOM. DAY
*A second dressing-table is covered with extravagant numbers of
perfume boxes.* MERTEUIL, *now in corset, chemise and underskirt,
sits, surrounded by her maids. Eventually she makes a choice and
indicates a box. A maid opens the box and begins to apply the
perfume (in the form of a cream) to* MERTEUIL*'s neck, lightly
massaging it in.*

INT. ANTEROOM TO VALMONT'S BEDROOM. DAY
Valmont's perruquier waits attentively as VALMONT, *seen from
behind, stands in front of the three tiers of featureless wooden
heads that carry his collection of wigs. Eventually, he points to
one.*

INT. MERTEUIL'S DRESSING-ROOM. DAY
MERTEUIL*'s stomacher is now in position and she stands, arms
outstretched, as two maids move forward with her dress, guiding
her arms into it as if it were an overcoat. This done, Merteuil's
seamstress approaches and begins the delicate process of sewing her
into her dress. The back of her dress is lifted so that one of her
maids can tighten her corset.*

INT. VALMONT'S BEDROOM. DAY
A bizarre paper cone with gauze-covered eyeholes conceals
VALMONT*'s face as the perruquier blows powder at his wig. As
the powder drifts away,* VALMONT *slowly lowers the cone and we
see for the first time his intelligent and malicious features.
Another angle shows the complete magnificent ensemble; or not
quite complete, for* AZOLAN *now reaches his arms round*
VALMONT*'s waist to strap on his sword.*

INT. CORRIDOR IN MERTEUIL'S HOUSE. DAY
MERTEUIL *emerges triumphally from her dressing-room, her expression serene.*

INT. VALMONT'S BEDROOM. DAY
VALMONT, *surrounded by his servants, frozen in postures of respectful silence, sets off with a spring in his step to begin his day's work.*

EXT. COURTYARD OF MERTEUIL'S TOWN HOUSE. DUSK
VALMONT's *handsome black carriage comes to a halt and he emerges, resplendent.*
Above, at the window, peering curiously down at VALMONT, *is a demure fifteen-year-old blonde,* CÉCILE VOLANGES.

INT. ANTEROOM TO THE GRAND SALON IN MERTEUIL'S HOUSE. DUSK
CÉCILE *turns away from the window, thoughtful.*

INT. MERTEUIL'S GRAND SALON. DUSK
A panoramic view of the great room. In one corner MERTEUIL *is playing piquet with her cousin* MADAME DE VOLANGES: *in the centre of the room, the huge chandelier has been lowered to within a foot of the floor and two footmen with tapers are lighting its candles.*
CÉCILE *moves across the room. The large playing cards slap down on one another.*
VOLANGES: Sequence.
> (MERTEUIL *looks across the long expanse of room at* CÉCILE's *profile. Eventually she speaks.*)
MERTEUIL: Well, my dear . . .
> (CÉCILE *doesn't at first realize it's she who's being addressed: then she starts and half turns.*)
So how are you adapting to the outside world?
CÉCILE: Very well. I think.
VOLANGES: I've advised her to watch and learn and be quiet except when spoken to.
> (MERTEUIL *looks* CÉCILE *up and down, frankly appraising her.*)

3

MERTEUIL: We must see what we can devise for your
amusement.

(*The mirrored double doors open and Merteuil's*
MAJORDOMO, *carrying a silver tray, advances unhurriedly*
across the room. The chandelier is fully lit now and the
footmen begin to raise it. MERTEUIL *glances up at her*
MAJORDOMO *and reaches for the card on his tray. She*
replaces the card, looks up at him and nods. Gradually, as
the chandelier rises, MERTEUIL's *perfect, mask-like face*
becomes fully lit.)

Valmont is here.

(VOLANGES *reacts with a trace of alarm.*)

VOLANGES: You receive him, do you?

MERTEUIL: Yes. So do you.

(VOLANGES *turns to her daughter, whose interest has been*
caught by this exchange.)

VOLANGES: Monsieur le Vicomte de Valmont, my child,
whom you very probably don't remember, except that he
is conspicuously charming, never opens his mouth without
first calculating what damage he can do.

CÉCILE: Then why do you receive him, maman?

VOLANGES: Everyone receives him.

(*She breaks off as the* MAJORDOMO *reappears, escorting*
VALMONT, *who crosses to bow formally to* MERTEUIL *in a*
gesture that also takes in the others.)

VALMONT: Madame.

MERTEUIL: Vicomte.

VOLANGES: What a pleasant surprise.

VALMONT: Madame de Volanges. How delightful to see you.

VOLANGES: You remember my daughter, Cécile?

VALMONT: Well, indeed, but who could have foretold she
would flower so gracefully?

(VOLANGES *is not best pleased by this remark;*
meanwhile VALMONT *turns his attention back to*
MERTEUIL.)

I wanted to call on you before leaving the city.

MERTEUIL: Oh, I'm not sure we can allow that. Why should
you want to leave?

VALMONT: Paris in August, you know; and it's time I paid a visit on my old aunt. I've neglected her disgracefully.

VOLANGES: Madame de Rosemonde has been good enough to invite us to stay at the château. Will you please give her our warmest regards?

VALMONT: I shall make a point of it, madame.

(VOLANGES, *made uneasy by* VALMONT's *professional scrutiny of* CÉCILE, *speaks to her daughter more sharply than she intends.*)

VOLANGES: I think it's time we took you home.

(CÉCILE *responds, still nervously aware of* VALMONT's *unwavering stare.*)

CÉCILE: I'm used to being in bed by nine at the convent.

VALMONT: So I should hope.

(*She breaks away, mysteriously alarmed, and hurries across to* VOLANGES. MERTEUIL *has summoned a footman.*
VALMONT *bows and we watch from his point of view as the footman shows out* VOLANGES *and* CÉCILE. *When they've gone,* MERTEUIL *crosses back towards* VALMONT, *speaking in an entirely different tone of voice.*)

MERTEUIL: Your aunt?

VALMONT: That's correct.

MERTEUIL: I thought she'd already made arrangements to leave you all her money.

(*He smiles without answering. She arrives beside him.*)
Do you know why I summoned you here this evening?

VALMONT: I'd hoped it might be for the pleasure of my company.

MERTEUIL: I need you; to carry out an heroic enterprise. You remember when Bastide left me?

(VALMONT *feigns a sympathetic expression.*)

VALMONT: Yes.

MERTEUIL: And went off with that fat mistress of yours whose name escapes me.

VALMONT: Yes, yes.

MERTEUIL: No one has ever done that to me before. Or to you, I imagine.

VALMONT: I was quite relieved to be rid of her, frankly.

MERTEUIL: No, you weren't.
(*Silence. She now has his undivided attention.*)
For some years now, Bastide has been searching for a
wife. He was always unshakeably prejudiced in favour of
convent education. And now he's found the ideal
candidate.

INT. CONVENT. DAY
CÉCILE, *superintended by a couple of nuns, waits inside an
enclosure, her face framed between the bars of a wooden partition.*
VALMONT: (*Voice over*) Cécile Volanges.
MERTEUIL: (*Voice over*) Very good.

EXT. CONVENT. DAY
VOLANGES's *magnificent carriage, silhouetted against the walls
of the convent.*
VALMONT: (*Voice over*) And her sixty thousand a year, that
must have played some part in his calculations.
(*A nun peeps through the grille in the gate of the convent.*)
MERTEUIL: (*Voice over*) None whatsoever.

INT. CONVENT. DAY
VOLANGES, *escorted by nuns, moves along a vaulted stone
corridor.*
MERTEUIL: (*Voice over*) His priority, you see, is a guaranteed
virtue.
VALMONT: (*Voice over*) I wonder if I'm beginning to guess
what it is you're intending to propose.
(VOLANGES *hasn't seen* CÉCILE *for years. She advances
tentatively towards the partition. Still on the other side of it,*
CÉCILE *curtsies respectfully.*)
MERTEUIL: (*Voice over*) Bastide is with his regiment in
Corsica for the rest of the year. That should give you
plenty of time.

INT. MERTEUIL'S GRAND SALON. DUSK
VALMONT *rises into frame.*
VALMONT: You mean to . . .?
(MERTEUIL *arrives at his shoulder.*)

6

MERTEUIL: She's a rosebud.

VALMONT: You think so?

MERTEUIL: And he'd get back from honeymoon to find himself the laughing-stock of Paris.

VALMONT: Well . . .

MERTEUIL: Yes. Love and revenge: two of your favourites. (*Silence.* VALMONT *considers for a moment. Finally, he shakes his head.*)

VALMONT: No, I can't.

MERTEUIL: What?

VALMONT: Really, I can't.

MERTEUIL: Why not?

VALMONT: It's too easy. It is. She's seen nothing, she knows nothing, she's bound to be curious, she'd be on her back before you'd unwrapped the first bunch of flowers. Any one of a dozen men could manage it. I have my reputation to think of.

(MERTEUIL *frowns, displeased.* VALMONT *moves over to sit next to her.*)

I can see I'm going to have to tell you everything.

MERTEUIL: Of course you are.

VALMONT: Yes. Well. My aunt is not on her own just at the moment. She has a young friend staying with her.

EXT. FORMAL GARDENS OF ROSEMONDE'S CHATEAU. DAY

MADAME DE TOURVEL's *strong, beautiful, untroubled face, as she moves through the gardens. She's accompanied by Valmont's eighty-year-old aunt,* MADAME DE ROSEMONDE, *who chooses flowers, which* TOURVEL *then cuts and lays in a basket.*

VALMONT: (*Voice over*) Madame de Tourvel.

INT. MERTEUIL'S GRAND SALON. DUSK

MERTEUIL *turns to him, genuinely surprised.*

MERTEUIL: You can't mean it.

VALMONT: To seduce a woman famous for strict morals, religious fervour and the happiness of her marriage: what could possibly be more prestigious?

7

MERTEUIL: I think there's something degrading about having a husband for a rival. It's humiliating if you fail and commonplace if you succeed.

EXT. ROSEMONDE'S GARDENS. DAY
TOURVEL *supports* ROSEMONDE *as they move back towards the château.*
MERTEUIL: (*Voice over*) Where is Monsieur de Tourvel anyway?
VALMONT: (*Voice over*) Presiding over some endless case in Burgundy.
MERTEUIL: (*Voice over*) I don't think you can hope for any actual pleasure.
VALMONT: (*Voice over*) Oh, yes.

INT. MERTEUIL'S GRAND SALON. DUSK
VALMONT *leans in, his tone more intimate.*
VALMONT: You see, I have no intention of breaking down her prejudices. I want her to believe in God and virtue and the sanctity of marriage and still not be able to stop herself. I want the excitement of watching her betray everything that's most important to her. Surely you understand that. I thought betrayal was your favourite word.
MERTEUIL: No, no, cruelty: I always think that has a nobler ring to it.
(*He contemplates her for a moment, lost in admiration.*)

INT. CORRIDOR OF MIRRORS. DUSK
The first-floor landing in MERTEUIL'*s house is an immense gallery of mirrors. She and* VALMONT *pass down the corridor, their images shifting and multiplying in the candlelight.*
VALMONT: How's Belleroche?
MERTEUIL: I'm very pleased with him.
VALMONT: And is he your only lover?
(MERTEUIL *pretends to give this a moment's consideration.*)
MERTEUIL: Yes.
VALMONT: I think you should take another. I think it most unhealthy, this exclusivity.

MERTEUIL: You're not jealous, are you?
VALMONT: Of course I am. Belleroche is completely
    undeserving.
MERTEUIL: I thought he was one of your closest friends.
VALMONT: Exactly, so I know what I'm talking about.

INT. LANDING. DUSK
VALMONT *and* MERTEUIL *emerge on to the landing at the top
of the broad and imposing staircase which leads down to the
entrance of the house.*
VALMONT: No, I think you should organize an infidelity.
    With me, for example.
    (MERTEUIL *stops and looks up at him, smiling.*)
MERTEUIL: You refuse me a simple favour and then you
    expect to be indulged?
VALMONT: It's only because it *is* so simple. It wouldn't feel
    like a conquest. I have to follow my destiny. I have to be
    true to my profession.

INT. STAIRCASE. DUSK
VALMONT *plants a chaste kiss on* MERTEUIL*'s bosom and sets
off down the stairs.* MERTEUIL*'s voice stops him in his tracks.*
MERTEUIL: All right, then: come back when you've succeeded
    with Madame de Tourvel.
VALMONT: Yes?
MERTEUIL: And I will offer you . . . a reward.
VALMONT: My love.
MERTEUIL: But I shall require proof.
VALMONT: Certainly.
MERTEUIL: Written proof.
VALMONT: Ah.
MERTEUIL: Not negotiable.
    (VALMONT *recovers quickly.*)
VALMONT: I don't suppose there's any possibility of an
    advance?
MERTEUIL: Goodnight, Vicomte.
    (*She grants him a dazzling smile and leaves him.*)

9

INT. CORRIDOR OF MIRRORS. DUSK
MERTEUIL *stops in front of one of the mirrors. It turns out to be a door, which she opens.*

INT. SPIRAL STAIRCASE. DUSK
A candle at the top sheds a dim light; MERTEUIL *begins to ascend her secret staircase.*

INT. MERTEUIL'S BEDROOM. DUSK
BELLEROCHE, *a beautiful blockhead of about thirty, springs to his feet as* MERTEUIL *emerges from what is ostensibly a cupboard door. He hurries over to embrace her.*
BELLEROCHE: Where have you been? Time has no logic when I'm not with you: an hour is like a century.
MERTEUIL: I've told you before: we shall get on a good deal better if you make a concerted effort not to sound like the latest novel.
(*She closes the door purposefully.*)

INT. PRIVATE CHAPEL IN ROSEMONDE'S GROUNDS. DAY
The sound of the little silver bell which summons the congregation to take Communion: close on TOURVEL *as her hands part to reveal her face.* ROSEMONDE *kneels next to her and is now being helped to her feet by* VALMONT.
VALMONT *escorts* ROSEMONDE *up the stairs to the altar rail,* TOURVEL *remaining on the other side of her. The rest of the congregation consists of Rosemonde's domestic staff, in a segregated portion of the chapel; and they file up towards the altar, respectfully waiting their turn.*
TOURVEL *kneels at the altar rail as* VALMONT *helps* ROSEMONDE *to kneel beside her. Then* TOURVEL *looks up, slightly surprised, as* VALMONT *moves off to one side, instead of taking his place at the rail. By now, the elderly Curé, intoning the Latin mass, is approaching* TOURVEL *with the large Communion wafer.* VALMONT *watches intently.*
VALMONT*'s point of view: the wafer is placed on* TOURVEL*'s lower lip and slowly vanishes into her mouth.*
TOURVEL*'s point of view:* VALMONT, *his expression respectful, his demeanour humble.*

EXT. ROSEMONDE'S PRIVATE CHAPEL. DAY
Beautiful summer's day. The chapel is in the grounds of
ROSEMONDE's *château, the turrets of which are visible in*
the distance. Her open carriage stands waiting, as the congregation
emerges into the sunlight. The coachman jumps down, but
ROSEMONDE *dismisses him with a gesture.*
ROSEMONDE: It's such a beautiful day, I believe we'll walk.
   (*A little way off,* TOURVEL *shyly approaches* VALMONT.)
TOURVEL: You didn't take the sacrament today.
VALMONT: No.
TOURVEL: May I ask why?
VALMONT: I have this appalling reputation, as you may
   know . . .
TOURVEL: Oh, yes, I have been warned about you.
VALMONT: You have? By whom?
TOURVEL: A friend.

EXT. GROUNDS OF ROSEMONDE'S CHATEAU. DAY
VALMONT *and* TOURVEL *stroll back across the sunlit lawns.*
VALMONT: The fact is I've spent my life surrounded by
   immoral people; I've allowed myself to be influenced by
   them and sometimes even taken pride in outshining them.
TOURVEL: And now?
VALMONT: Now what I feel most often is unworthiness.
TOURVEL: But it's precisely at such moments you start to
   become worthy.
   (VALMONT *appears to give this assertion his serious*
   consideration. He glances back to see AZOLAN, *who is*
   flirting with Tourvel's young chambermaid, JULIE)
VALMONT: I certainly believe that one should constantly
   strive to improve oneself.
   (*Long shot: the two of them among the entire household,*
   moving back towards the austere and massively imposing
   shape of the château, as, on sound, the passionate climax of
   the aria 'O malheureuse Iphigénie' from Gluck's Iphigénie
   en Tauride *begins to swell.*)

INT. MERTEUIL'S BOX AT THE OPERA. EVENING
The aria continues; the opera is in progress. VOLANGES *and*

CÉCILE, *in the box, stare down at the stage.* MERTEUIL, *however, opera glasses pressed to her face, is scanning the audience.*

INT. OPERA HOUSE. EVENING
MERTEUIL'*s point of view, as her gaze comes to rest on the face of a handsome young man of not more than twenty, listening intently, tears streaming down his face: the* CHEVALIER DANCENY.

INT. MERTEUIL'S BOX. EVENING
A knock at the door and DANCENY, *charmingly shy and uncertain, bows deeply to* MERTEUIL.
MERTEUIL: Chevalier, I don't believe you know my cousin, Madame de Volanges. This is Chevalier Danceny. And madame's daughter, Cécile.
   (*All this has taken place very quickly and now* DANCENY *becomes aware of* CÉCILE *for the first time: he looks at her, tongue-tied, obviously smitten, eventually managing to utter a strangled greeting.* MERTEUIL *observes him shrewdly.*)
   Tell us what we should think of the opera.
DANCENY: Oh, it's sublime. Don't you find?
MERTEUIL: Monsieur Danceny is one of those rare eccentrics who come here to listen to the music.
DANCENY: I do look forward to our next meeting.
   (*He bows to* CÉCILE, *blushing deeply, and leaves the box.* CÉCILE'*s eyes are shining.* MERTEUIL *is watching her closely.*)
MERTEUIL: Charming young man. Penniless, regrettably. He's one of the finest music teachers in the city.
   (*Close on* CÉCILE: *the idea occurs to her at the very moment* MERTEUIL *expresses it.*)
   Perhaps you should employ him.

EXT. ROSEMONDE'S CHATEAU. DAWN
JULIE *steps out on to the balcony of* TOURVEL'*s room.*

EXT. COURTYARD AT ROSEMONDE'S CHATEAU. DAWN
Below, VALMONT *and* AZOLAN, *who carries a long musket over his shoulder, descend a staircase and crunch across the gravel. Another angle reveals a figure in stealthy pursuit of them: Tourvel's footman,* GEORGES.

INT. TOURVEL'S BEDROOM. DAWN
JULIE *comes in from the balcony and bends to wake* TOURVEL *and murmur in her ear.*

EXT. WOODS. DAWN
VALMONT *and* AZOLAN *stride through the waist-high grass.*
VALMONT: How are you getting on with Madame de Tourvel's maid?
AZOLAN: Julie? Tell you the truth, it's been a bit boring. If I wasn't so anxious to keep your lordship abreast, I think I'd have only bothered the once. Still, you know, what else is there to do in the country?
VALMONT: Yes, it wasn't so much the details of your intimacy I was after, it was whether she's agreed to bring me Madame de Tourvel's letters.
AZOLAN: She won't steal the letters, sir.
VALMONT: She won't?
AZOLAN: You know better than me, sir, it's easy enough making them do what they want to do; it's trying to get them to do what you want them to do, that's what gives you a headache.
VALMONT: And them, as often as not. I need to know who's writing to her about me.
AZOLAN: I shouldn't worry if I was you, sir. She told Julie she didn't believe you went hunting in the mornings. She said she was going to have you followed. So I'd say it was only a matter of time.
(*They carry on through the woods. Behind them,* GEORGES *blunders incompetently from tree to tree.*)

EXT. BOUNDARY OF ROSEMONDE'S LAND. DAY
AZOLAN *unlocks a gate in the wall enclosing* ROSEMONDE'S

13

property to let VALMONT *through. The latter hesitates, looking back.*

VALMONT: Terrible noise he's making.

AZOLAN: He should get the news back to her twice as quickly.

VALMONT: I don't think we should make it too easy for him.
> (*He takes the musket from* AZOLAN *and suddenly fires it into the undergrowth.*)

EXT. UNDERGROWTH. DAY
GEORGES, *panic-stricken, hurls himself to the ground as the echoes of the shot die away.*

EXT. VILLAGE SQUARE. DAY
The village consists of half-a-dozen wattle-and-daub huts disposed around a muddy clearing, where pigs graze and barefoot children wander. The poverty is as stark and absolute as that of a village in India. A small crowd is gathered around one of the huts,
ARMAND's, *out of which a couple of men, supervised by the* BAILIFF, *are carrying a plain deal table, which they dump down next to three wooden chairs. A gaunt woman follows them, miserably wringing her hands.*

VALMONT *and* AZOLAN *arrive: the former takes in the situation and turns to confront the* BAILIFF.

VALMONT: What exactly do you think you're doing?

BAILIFF: I am impounding these effects, sir.

VALMONT: Has it not been explained to you? Monsieur Armand is not well.

BAILIFF: I don't make the laws, sir, I just do what I'm told. Everybody has to pay his taxes.

VALMONT: How much does he owe?

BAILIFF: Well . . .

VALMONT: How much?

BAILIFF: Fifty-six livres.
> (VALMONT *takes a large, jingling purse out of his pocket and hands it to* AZOLAN.)

VALMONT: Pay him.

AZOLAN: Yes, my lord.
> (VALMONT *ducks into* ARMAND's *hut, as* GEORGES *arrives on the fringes of the crowd and hurries to* ARMAND's *window.*)

14

INT. ARMAND'S HUT. DAY

GEORGES's *point of view:* VALMONT *stands looking down at* ARMAND, *a man of not more than fifty, who looks ancient, gnarled and battered by work, his hair long, thick and white.*

VALMONT: Monsieur Armand. You don't know me.

ARMAND: Of course I do, Monsieur le Vicomte.

VALMONT: Please, don't get up.

(ARMAND *is struggling up out of his large pallet bed covered with sacking.*)

ARMAND: I have to, sir. They're taking the bed.

VALMONT: Not at all. No one is taking anything.

EXT. VILLAGE SQUARE. DAY

VALMONT *leaves the hut, pursued by* ARMAND, *who falls to his knees to kiss* VALMONT's *hand, as his wife (the gaunt woman) embraces* VALMONT's *other hand.*

VALMONT: Azolan.

(*Another angle shows* VALMONT *and* AZOLAN *surrounded by villagers and their children.* VALMONT *distributes gold coins to the clamouring crowd.*)

Just to tide you over. I insist.

EXT. BOUNDARY OF ROSEMONDE'S LAND. DAY

AZOLAN *unlocks a compartment in one of the brick gateposts and takes out a wooden mailbox with a slot in the top. Then he takes a pin from his wig and begins delicately to probe the lock of the mailbox as they talk.*

VALMONT: Fifty-six livres to save an entire family from ruin, that seems a genuine bargain.

AZOLAN: These days, my lord, you can find half a dozen like that, any village in the country.

VALMONT: Really? I must say the family was very well chosen. Solidly respectable, gratifyingly tearful, no suspiciously pretty girls. Well done.

AZOLAN: I do my best for you, sir.

VALMONT: And all that humble gratitude. It was most affecting.

AZOLAN: Certainly brought a tear to my eye.

(*The lock yields to his manipulations, the mailbox opens and after a brief inspection he hands two letters to* VALMONT, *who glances at the postmarks and hands one of them straight back to* AZOLAN.)

VALMONT: Dijon. That's from her husband.

(*He holds the other letter, which is in a distinctive, somewhat pretentious envelope, up to the light.*)

This must be from that officious friend of hers.

(*He passes it back to* AZOLAN, *who returns it to the mailbox and closes it. They move off, back in the direction of the house.*)

Tell me, where do you and Julie meet?

AZOLAN: Oh, in my room, sir.

(AZOLAN *unlocks the gate and they pass through it.*)

VALMONT: And is she coming tonight?

AZOLAN: Afraid so.

VALMONT: Then I think I may have to burst in on you. See if blackmail will succeed better than bribery. About two o'clock suit you? I don't want to embarrass you, will that give you enough time?

AZOLAN: Ample, sir.

INT. GRAND SALON IN ROSEMONDE'S CHATEAU. DAY

VALMONT *looks up from his book, as* ROSEMONDE *bustles into the room, followed by* TOURVEL. *He rises to greet them.*

ROSEMONDE: Is this true about Monsieur Armand?

VALMONT: I don't believe I know anyone of that name . . .

TOURVEL: You may as well own up, monsieur. My footman happened to be passing when you were in the village this morning.

VALMONT: I don't think you ought to pay too much attention to servants' gossip.

ROSEMONDE: It is true, isn't it?

VALMONT: Well, I . . . Yes, it is.

(*He looks up, ostensibly deeply embarrassed, to catch* TOUR-VEL'*s admiring gaze.* ROSEMONDE *spreads her arms.*)

ROSEMONDE: You dear boy, come and let me give you a hug!

(VALMONT *crosses to her and they embrace. Then* VALMONT *turns and advances towards* TOURVEL. *Before*

16

*she can escape, he's embraced her and, for a second, she's in
his arms. Meanwhile Rosemonde's steward has entered, with
the mail laid out on a salver. As* TOURVEL *escapes from*
VALMONT*'s arms, she finds the steward at her elbow.
Ashen, she shakily reaches out her hand for the two letters.)*

INT. GRAND SALON IN ROSEMONDE'S CHATEAU. NIGHT
VALMONT *is reading and* TOURVEL *is looking over her letter
from Paris, the one with the distinctive envelope. Eventually, she
looks up at him and breaks the silence.*

TOURVEL: I can't understand how someone whose instincts
are so generous could lead such a dissolute life.

VALMONT: I'm afraid you have an exaggerated idea both of
my generosity and of my depravity. If I knew who'd given
you such a dire account of me . . .
(TOURVEL *folds up her letter, her expression sheepish.*)
. . . since I don't, let me make a confession. I'm afraid
the key to the paradox lies in a certain weakness of
character.

TOURVEL: I can't see how so thoughtful an act of charity
could be described as weak.

VALMONT: Because it was simply a response to a strong new
influence in my life: yours.
(TOURVEL *looks away.* VALMONT *sighs.*)
You see how weak I am? I promised myself I was never
going to tell you. It's just, looking at you . . .

TOURVEL: Monsieur.

VALMONT: You needn't worry, I have no illicit intentions. I
wouldn't dream of insulting you. But I do love you. I
adore you.
(*The letter slips from* TOURVEL*'s fingers.* VALMONT *is
across the room in an instant, on his knees in front of her,
handing her the letter and then taking her hand in his.*)
Please help me.
(TOURVEL *scrambles to her feet, horrified, and begins to
move away across the great room, her pace increasing as she
realizes that* VALMONT *is pursuing her.*)

INT. MAIN STAIRCASE. NIGHT
TOURVEL *hurries up the vast, wide staircase. Below,* VALMONT, *in pursuit, emerges into the hallway.*

INT. CORRIDOR. NIGHT
TOURVEL*'s back recedes down the corridor. Presently,* VALMONT *comes into frame, catching her up. But* TOURVEL *disappears into her room and there's the sound of a heavy bolt.* VALMONT *arrives at her door and drops to his knees, pressing his eye to her keyhole.*

INT. TOURVEL'S BEDROOM. NIGHT
Keyhole shot: TOURVEL, *panting, distressed, begins to loosen her bodice.*

INT. CORRIDOR. NIGHT
VALMONT *stands up. There's a look of satisfaction on his face as he begins to tiptoe away.*

INT. AZOLAN'S BEDROOM. NIGHT
AZOLAN *is in bed with* JULIE, *they're asleep in each other's arms. Suddenly the door bursts open.* VALMONT *stands in the doorway in his dressing-gown, holding a candlestick. In its flickering light,* AZOLAN *and* JULIE *wake,* JULIE *genuinely terrified and* AZOLAN *(since this has been prearranged) convincingly dismayed.*
VALMONT: I rang a number of times.
AZOLAN: Didn't hear, sir.
VALMONT: I require some hot water.
AZOLAN: Right away, sir.
> (*He jumps out of bed, uncovering* JULIE. *She reaches for the sheets but* VALMONT *speaks sharply, stopping her in her tracks.*)
VALMONT: Don't move.
> (*As* AZOLAN *puts on a dressing-gown and hurries to the door,* VALMONT *settles himself on the end of the bed, his eyes burning into* JULIE.)
Azolan.

AZOLAN: Sir.

VALMONT: Wait for me in my room.

> (AZOLAN *hurries out.* VALMONT *continues to stare at*
> JULIE, *who is becoming increasingly uncomfortable.*)

You know I can't condone this sort of behaviour, Julie.

JULIE: I know, sir . . .

VALMONT: But you may rely on my discretion . . .

JULIE: Oh, thank you, sir.

VALMONT: . . . providing, of course, that you agree to my
price.

> (*There's a silence, during which* JULIE *thinks she understands*
> *what he means. Her expression changes as she tries to work*
> *out how best to react. But* VALMONT *shakes his head.*)

No, no, nothing like that. No, all I want is to see every
letter Madame de Tourvel has received since her arrival
here and every letter she writes from now on.

JULIE: But, sir . . .

VALMONT: Deliver them to Azolan by midnight tomorrow.

> (*He stands, continuing to look at her for a moment, until she*
> *snatches at the sheet and covers herself. He brings a handful*
> *of gold coins out of his dressing-gown pocket and pours them*
> *on to the bed.*)

For your trouble.

INT. CORRIDOR OUTSIDE AZOLAN'S BEDROOM. NIGHT
AZOLAN *is waiting outside the door.* VALMONT *gives him his*
candle to hold, while he gathers up the train of his dressing-gown.
This done, he takes back the candlestick and begins his descent
from the attic floor of the château.

INT. GRAND SALON IN MERTEUIL'S HOUSE. DAY
CÉCILE *is playing the harp and singing an aria from Gluck's*
Paride e Elena, *accompanied on the harpsichord by* DANCENY.
On the far side of the room, VOLANGES *is a benevolent spectator.*
After a time, DANCENY *breaks off, hitting a note several times to*
indicate where CÉCILE's *voice has gone wrong. They resume a*
few bars back; this time CÉCILE *gets it right and* DANCENY *nods*
in approval. They proceed until CÉCILE *makes a mistake with*

the harp. DANCENY, *seeing that* VOLANGES*'s back is now turned, crosses, takes* CÉCILE*'s hands and adjusts them to the correct position. Then, he takes the opportunity to slip a piece of paper between the harp strings. She frowns and then unfolds it. It contains the message:* I LOVE YOU.

MERTEUIL *arrives in the room, smiling hospitably at* VOLANGES. CÉCILE *darts a furious glance at* DANCENY. *Then they resume playing and singing.*

MERTEUIL *winces, closing her eyes as if to blot out the cacophony.*

INT. MERTEUIL'S BOX AT THE OPERA. EVENING
MERTEUIL *and* CÉCILE *are attending a performance of* Paride e Elena. CÉCILE, *evidently in some distress, turns to appeal to* MERTEUIL.

CÉCILE: Would it be very wrong of me to answer Monsieur Danceny's letters?

MERTEUIL: In the circumstances, yes.

CÉCILE: In what circumstances?

(MERTEUIL *pretends to reflect before answering.*)

MERTEUIL: It's not my place to tell you this, my dear . . . if I hadn't become so fond of you . . .

CÉCILE: Go on, please!

MERTEUIL: Your marriage has been arranged.

CÉCILE: Who is it?

MERTEUIL: Someone I know, slightly. Monsieur le Comte de Bastide.

CÉCILE: What's he like?

MERTEUIL: Well . . .

CÉCILE: You don't like him.

MERTEUIL: It's not that. He's a man of somewhat . . . erratic judgement. And rather serious.

CÉCILE: How old is he?

MERTEUIL: Thirty-six.

CÉCILE: Thirty-six? He's an old man!

(MERTEUIL *smiles, as another thought galvanizes* CÉCILE.)
Do you know when?

MERTEUIL: In the new year, I believe.

(*She stares, unseeing, at the stage, lost in thought.*
MERTEUIL *leans in closer to her.*)
Perhaps there is a way to let you write to Monsieur
Danceny . . .
CÉCILE: Oh, madame!
(*She's caught hold of* MERTEUIL*'s hand, her eyes shining.*)
MERTEUIL: If you were to let me see both sides of the
correspondence, I could reassure myself . . .
(CÉCILE *throws herself into* MERTEUIL*'s arms and embraces
her.* MERTEUIL*'s eyes glitter in the darkness. Then* CÉCILE
looks up at her.)
CÉCILE: I can't show you the letters I've already sent him . . .
(*She breaks off, realizing she's given herself away, her
expression apprehensive. But* MERTEUIL*'s smile is indulgent.
As the impassioned love duet on stage reaches a climax, she
stretches out a hand to caress* CÉCILE*'s neck and collarbone.*)

EXT. GARDENS OF ROSEMONDE'S CHATEAU. DAY
TOURVEL *moves down a path in a secluded part of the gardens.
She becomes aware, too late for evasion, that* VALMONT *is
approaching down a separate but intersecting path. He speaks as
he intercepts her.*
VALMONT: I trust you slept well. I wish I could say that I had.
TOURVEL: I thought the least I could hope for was that you
would respect me.
VALMONT: But I do, of course I do.
TOURVEL: You've offended me deeply, it's unforgivable. This
confirms everything I've been told about you. I'm
beginning to think you may have planned the whole
exercise.
(*She turns and moves briskly away, obliging him to hurry
after her.*)
VALMONT: I had no idea you were staying here. Not that it
would have disturbed me in the slightest if I had known.
You see, until I met you, I had only ever experienced
desire. Love, never.
(*He has succeeded in stopping her with his eloquence. Now
she moves away again, offended.*)

21

TOURVEL: That's enough.

(*He pursues her, talking fast.*)

VALMONT: No, no, you made an accusation, you must allow me the opportunity to defend myself. Now I'm not going to deny that I was aware of your beauty . . .

TOURVEL: Monsieur.

VALMONT: . . . but the point is, all this has nothing to do with your beauty. As I got to know you, I began to realize that beauty was the least of your qualities. I became fascinated by your goodness. I was drawn in by it. I didn't understand what was happening to me and it was only when I began to feel actual physical pain every time you left the room, that it finally dawned on me: I was in love, for the first time in my life.

(TOURVEL *quickens her pace.*)

I knew it was hopeless, but that didn't matter to me; and it's not that I want to have you . . .

(*He succeeds in stopping her short.*)

. . . all I want is to deserve you. Tell me what to do, show me how to behave, I'll do anything you say.

TOURVEL: Very well, then. I would like you to leave this house.

VALMONT: I don't see why that should be necessary.

TOURVEL: Let's just say you've spent your whole life making it necessary. And if you refuse, I shall be forced to leave myself.

VALMONT: Well, then, of course, whatever you say.

TOURVEL: Thank you.

(*She moves away again, leaving* VALMONT *temporarily bested. He lets her go two or three steps, before setting off in pursuit.*)

VALMONT: Perhaps I might be so bold as to ask a favour in return. I think it would only be just to let me know which of your friends has blackened my name.

TOURVEL: If friends of mine have warned me against you, I can hardly reward them with betrayal. I must say you devalue your generous offer if you want to use it as a bargaining point.

VALMONT: Very well, I withdraw the request. I hope you won't think I'm bargaining if I ask you to let me write to you?

TOURVEL: Well . . .

VALMONT: And pray that you will do me the kindness of answering my letters?

(*He follows her, weaving from side to side, confusing her.*)

TOURVEL: I'm not sure a correspondence with you is something a woman of honour could permit herself.

VALMONT: So you're determined to refuse my suggestions, however respectable?

TOURVEL: I didn't say that . . .

VALMONT: And you'd rather be unjust than risk showing me a touch of kindness?

TOURVEL: I would welcome the chance to prove to you that what lies behind this is not hatred or resentment but . . .

VALMONT: But what?

(TOURVEL *seems unable to find a satisfactory answer to this. She moves away, leaving* VALMONT *pensive and not wholly displeased with the encounter.*)

INT. CORRIDOR OUTSIDE AZOLAN'S ROOM. NIGHT
JULIE *comes up the attic stairs holding a bundle of letters. She knocks on the door and* AZOLAN *opens it. She hands him the letters and he lets her into the room. He makes a wry face and closes the door behind her.*

INT. VALMONT'S BEDROOM. NIGHT
VALMONT *sits on his bed, inspecting one of the letters.* AZOLAN *stands beside him, holding a candle, his expression complacent.*

VALMONT: Listen to this: 'He knows exactly how far he may venture without risk and guarantees his own security by tormenting only the safest kind of victim: women.'

(*He turns the letter over and reads out the signature, nodding grimly.*)

VALMONT: Madame de Volanges.

EXT. MAIN ENTRANCE TO ROSEMONDE'S CHATEAU. DAY
VALMONT *embraces* ROSEMONDE *as his big black carriage waits at the foot of a flight of outside steps.*
VALMONT: Goodbye, aunt.
ROSEMONDE: Goodbye, dear boy.
> (*He moves across to* TOURVEL, *who waits nearby, kisses her hand and keeps hold of it a little too long. She speaks in an undertone.*)

TOURVEL: Monsieur, please . . .
VALMONT: I'll write soon.
> (*To her alarm, he leans forward and kisses her on the cheek. Then he turns and moves down through lines of liveried servants towards his carriage.*)

INT. ÉMILIE'S BEDROOM. NIGHT
A sheet of writing paper is spread across the bare back of ÉMILIE, *a courtesan, lying on her luxurious canopied bed.* VALMONT *perches a china inkwell on one of her buttocks and begins to write. Outside, there are occasional rumbles of thunder and flashes of lightning.*
VALMONT: 'My dear Madame de Tourvel . . . I have just come . . .'
> (ÉMILIE *laughs and turns to look back at him.*)

Don't move, I said . . . 'to my desk, in the middle of a stormy night; during which I have been . . . tossed . . .'

EXT. GARDENS OF ROSEMONDE'S CHATEAU. DAY
TOURVEL *sits on a bench, reading Valmont's letter.*
VALMONT: (*Voice over*) '. . . from exaltation to exhaustion and back again; yet despite these torments I guarantee that at this moment I am far happier than you . . .'
> (*The letter: a teardrop falls on to the paper, smudging the ink.*)

INT. ÉMILIE'S BEDROOM. NIGHT
VALMONT *lays aside paper, pen and inkwell and murmurs to* ÉMILIE.
VALMONT: We'll finish it later, shall we?
> (*He leans in to embrace her.*)

INT. GRAND SALON IN MERTEUIL'S HOUSE. DAY
MERTEUIL *stirs her tea, listening attentively. Her guest is the*
VICOMTE DE VALMONT. *It's September now and there's a*
hint of autumn in the afternoon light.

VALMONT: Your damned cousin, the Volanges bitch, wanted
me away from Madame de Tourvel: well, now I am and I
intend to make her suffer for it. Your plan to ruin her
daughter, are you making any progress? Is there anything
I can do to help? I'm entirely at your disposal.

MERTEUIL: Well, yes, I told Danceny you would act as his
confidant and adviser. I want you to stiffen his resolve, if
that's the phrase.
(VALMONT *frowns, not at all pleased.*)
I thought if anyone could help him . . .

VALMONT: Help? He doesn't need help, he needs hindrances:
if he has to climb over enough of them, he might
inadvertently fall on top of her.
(*He shakes his head dismissively, and moves over to flop*
down beside her on the sofa.)
I take it he hasn't been a great success.

MERTEUIL: He's been disastrous. Like most intellectuals, he's
intensely stupid.
(VALMONT *enjoys this: he looks at* MERTEUIL, *shaking his*
head in admiration.)

VALMONT: I often wonder how you managed to invent
yourself.

MERTEUIL: I had no choice, did I? I'm a woman. Women are
obliged to be far more skilful than men. You can ruin our
reputation and our life with a few well-chosen words. So
of course I had to invent: not only myself but ways of
escape no one has ever thought of. And I've succeeded,
because I've always known I was born to dominate your
sex and avenge my own.

VALMONT: Yes; but what I asked you was how.

MERTEUIL: When I came out into society, I was fifteen. I
already knew that the role I was condemned to, namely to
keep quiet and do what I was told, gave me the perfect
opportunity to listen and pay attention: not to what people

told me, which was naturally of no interest, but to whatever it was they were trying to hide. I practised detachment. I learned how to look cheerful, while under the table I stuck a fork into the back of my hand. I became a virtuoso of deceit. It wasn't pleasure I was after, it was knowledge. I consulted the strictest moralists to learn how to appear, philosophers to find out what to think and novelists to see what I could get away with. And, in the end, I distilled everything down to one wonderfully simple principle: win or die.

VALMONT: So you're infallible, are you?

MERTEUIL: When I want a man, I have him; when he wants to tell, he finds he can't. That's the whole story.

VALMONT: And was that our story?

(MERTEUIL *pauses before answering: the air is becoming increasingly charged with eroticism.*)

MERTEUIL: I wanted you before we'd even met. My self-esteem demanded it. Then, when you began to pursue me, I wanted you so badly. It's the only time I've ever been controlled by my desire. Single combat.

(VALMONT *slides down the sofa towards her; but a heavy silence is interrupted by the arrival of Merteuil's* MAJOR-DOMO, *who murmurs into her ear.*)

MAJORDOMO: Madame de Volanges.

(MERTEUIL *is delighted.*)

MERTEUIL: Ah, Madame de Volanges.

INT. MAIN STAIRCASE. DAY

The MAJORDOMO *escorts an anxious-looking* VOLANGES *up the stairs.*

INT. GRAND SALON. DAY

VOLANGES *is shown into the great room. No sign of* VALMONT.

VOLANGES: Your note said it was urgent . . .

MERTEUIL: It's days now, I haven't been able to think of anything else. Please sit down.

(VOLANGES *subsides on to the sofa, thoroughly alarmed.*)

I have reason to believe that a, how can I describe it, a

dangerous liaison has sprung up between your daughter and the Chevalier Danceny.

(*A pan reveals, in the other half of the room, behind a screen,* VALMONT, *who is eavesdropping, bemused; he shakes his head, at a loss to understand* MERTEUIL*'s tactics. Meanwhile,* VOLANGES *is confidently dismissing the suggestion.*)

VOLANGES: No, no, that's completely absurd. Cécile is still a child, she understands nothing of these things; and Danceny is an entirely respectable young man.

MERTEUIL: Tell me, does Cécile have a great many correspondents?

VOLANGES: Why do you ask?

MERTEUIL: I went into her room at the beginning of this week, I simply knocked and entered; and she was stuffing a letter into the right-hand drawer of her bureau: in which, I couldn't help noticing, there seemed to be a large number of similar letters.

(*Silence. Behind the screen,* VALMONT*'s mouth is open in admiration and amazement.* VOLANGES *rises to her feet.*)

VOLANGES: I'm most grateful to you.

(MERTEUIL *rings, unable to resist a smile at the ease of it all.* VOLANGES *stands up, still in a state of mild shock.*)

MERTEUIL: Would you think it impertinent if I were to make another suggestion?

VOLANGES: No, no.

MERTEUIL: If my recollection is correct, I overheard you saying to the Vicomte de Valmont that his aunt had invited you and Cécile to stay at her château.

(VALMONT *stands on a chair to look over the screen at* MERTEUIL *and convey his displeasure at this turn of events.*)

VOLANGES: She has, yes, repeatedly.

(MERTEUIL *shoots a warning glance at* VALMONT.)

MERTEUIL: A spell in the country might be the very thing.

(VALMONT *has withdrawn; but now realizes he is visible in one of Merteuil's enormous mirrors and is obliged to dive full-length to escape detection. The* MAJORDOMO *hovers, waiting to show* VOLANGES *out; she turns back in the doorway, bowed down with care, her expression piteous.*)

VOLANGES: Thank you.

(*She leaves, and* MERTEUIL *turns back to* VALMONT, *triumphant. He is lost in admiration.*)

MERTEUIL: You asked for hindrances.

VALMONT: You are a genuinely wicked woman.

MERTEUIL: And you wanted a chance to make my cousin suffer.

VALMONT: I can't resist you.

MERTEUIL: I've made it easy for you.

VALMONT: But all this is most inconvenient; the Comtesse de Beaulieu has invited me to stay.

MERTEUIL: Well, you'll have to put her off.

VALMONT: The Comtesse has promised me extensive use of her gardens. It seems her husband's fingers are not as green as they once were.

MERTEUIL: Maybe not. But from what I hear, all his friends are gardeners.

VALMONT: Is that so?

MERTEUIL: You want your revenge. I want my revenge. I'm afraid there's really only one place you can go.

VALMONT: Back to Auntie, eh?

MERTEUIL: Back to Auntie. Where you can also pursue that other matter. You have some evidence to procure, have you not?

(VALMONT *doesn't answer for a moment. He approaches, reverting to the tone of just before* VOLANGES*'s arrival.*)

VALMONT: Don't you think it would be a generous gesture, show a proper confidence in my abilities, to take that evidence for granted . . . ?

MERTEUIL: I need it in writing, Vicomte.

(*He's close to her now, giving her his most charming smile. She leans her head back, unmoved. Their voices are intimate, his persuasive, hers amused.*)

And now you must leave me.

VALMONT: Must I? Why?

MERTEUIL: Because I'm hungry.

VALMONT: Yes, I've quite an appetite myself.

MERTEUIL: Then go home and eat.

(He leans in to kiss her, but she turns aside, offering him her cheek.)
In writing.
(He gives up, smiling at her, still in admiration.
Long shot: the two of them move across the vast room, exiting by different doors.)

INT. CÉCILE'S BEDROOM IN VOLANGES'S HOUSE. DAY
CÉCILE *looks up with a start as* VOLANGES *storms into the room, goes straight to her bureau and opens the right-hand drawer. Her eyes widen in horror as* VOLANGES *brings out a handful of letters.* VOLANGES *opens one of them, reads a sentence or two and looks up at* CÉCILE, *outraged.* CÉCILE *crumples to the floor in a dead faint.*

INT. GRAND SALON IN ROSEMONDE'S CHATEAU. DAY
VALMONT *is holding a sealed letter behind his back. He moves past* TOURVEL, *who sits staring, ashen, at a book; he pauses by* CÉCILE, *who sits in a windowseat, busy with her embroidery, and waves the letter at her, but she fails to understand and he is obliged to move on; past* VOLANGES *in the other windowseat; finally drifting by* ROSEMONDE, *who is playing solitaire at her card table. Now he's back where he started, his eyes fixed on* TOURVEL, *who glances up at him resentfully.* VOLANGES *arrives behind him, startling him as she snaps open her fan, but her position gives him another opportunity to display the letter to a still-puzzled* CÉCILE.
ROSEMONDE: You'll be pleased to hear, my dear, that Armand is on his feet again and back at work.
VALMONT: Who?
ROSEMONDE: Monsieur Armand, whose family you helped so generously.
VALMONT: Oh, yes.
*(*ROSEMONDE *turns to address* VOLANGES.*)*
ROSEMONDE: When my nephew was last staying here, we discovered quite by chance . . .
*(*VALMONT *interrupts her, suddenly rising to his feet, looking across at* TOURVEL.*)*

VALMONT: Are you feeling all right, madame? I'm sorry to interrupt you, Aunt, it seemed to me all of a sudden that Madame de Tourvel didn't look at all well.

TOURVEL: I'm . . . no, I'm quite all right.

(*By now,* ROSEMONDE *and* VOLANGES *are on their feet, converging on* TOURVEL.)

VOLANGES: Perhaps you need some air. Do you feel constricted in any way?

TOURVEL: No, really . . .

VALMONT: I feel sure Madame de Volanges is right, as usual. A turn around the grounds perhaps.

ROSEMONDE: Yes, yes, a little walk in the gardens; it's not too cool, I think.

(VALMONT *takes advantage of the confusion to throw the letter to* CÉCILE, *landing it neatly in her embroidery box, which she has the presence of mind to close. Meanwhile,* ROSEMONDE *and* VOLANGES *are shepherding a bewildered* TOURVEL *towards the french windows.*)

Fresh air will do you the world of good.

VOLANGES: The meal was somewhat heavy, perhaps . . .

ROSEMONDE: I don't believe that was the cause . . .

(*During this exchange,* CÉCILE *has gathered up her shawl and made to follow the others. As she's spreading it across her shoulders, however, she's startled to find it tugged away from her by* VALMONT, *who drops it on a chair, murmuring between clenched teeth.*)

VALMONT: Come back for it.

(*She frowns at him for a moment, then follows the still-clucking ladies out into the garden.* VALMONT *waits, by the window; presently* CÉCILE *hurries back into the room, not immediately seeing* VALMONT.)

Mademoiselle: I've no wish to arouse suspicion, so I'll be brief. The letter is from the Chevalier Danceny.

CÉCILE: Yes, I thought . . .

VALMONT: Now, the handing over of such letters is a far from easy matter to accomplish. I can't be expected to create a diversion every day. So . . .

(*He produces a large key.*)

This key resembles the key to your bedroom, which I happen to know is kept in your mother's bedroom, on the mantelpiece, tied with a blue ribbon. Take it, go up now, attach the blue ribbon to it and put it in place of your bedroom key, which you will then bring to me. I'll be able to get a copy cut within two hours. Then I'll be able to collect your letters and deliver Danceny's without any complications.
(*He puts the key into* CÉCILE*'s hand.*)
Oh, and in the cupboard by your bed, you'll find a feather and a small bottle of oil, so that you may oil the lock and hinges on the anteroom door.
(*He points towards the door.*)
CÉCILE: Are you sure, monsieur?
VALMONT: Trust me.
(CÉCILE *curtsies to him and begins to move away.*)
Believe me, mademoiselle, if there's one thing I can't abide, it's deceitfulness.
(*He watches her as she hurries away.*)

EXT. TERRACE. DAY
VALMONT *emerges from the french windows and pauses on the top step. Below, on the terrace, are* ROSEMONDE, VOLANGES *and* TOURVEL.

INT. VOLANGES'S BEDROOM. DAY
CÉCILE *finds the key on the mantelpiece and begins grappling with the blue ribbon.*

EXT. TERRACE. DAY
VALMONT *is now at the bottom of the steps. He calls out to* TOURVEL, *who's walking away with* VOLANGES.
VALMONT: I trust you're feeling a little better, madame.
(ROSEMONDE *watches from a nearby bench, her expression shrewd, as* TOURVEL *bears down on* VALMONT, *speaking in a fierce undertone.*)
TOURVEL: If I were ill, monsieur, it would not be difficult to guess who was responsible.

VALMONT: You can't mean me. Do you?
TOURVEL: You promised to leave here.
VALMONT: And I did.
(VALMONT *suddenly becomes aware that* VOLANGES *is heading purposefully back into the house.*)
Would you excuse me, madame?
(*He breaks away from her and hurries off up the stairs.*)

INT. GRAND SALON. DAY
VOLANGES *bustles in through the french windows. Behind, unseen by her,* VALMONT *follows, slipping across the room and out by a different door.*

INT. VOLANGES'S BEDROOM. DAY
CÉCILE *has almost finished tying the blue ribbon on to the second key, when she's startled by the sound of the creaking anteroom door. The key slips from her fingers and drops into a tall china vase in the grate. She drops to her knees to retrieve it, but the neck of the vase is too narrow to admit her hand. As she struggles with it,* VALMONT *appears in the doorway.*
VALMONT: Quick. Your mother.
(*He hurries across to her, assessing the situation in a flash, picks up the vase and inverts it, emptying the key into* CÉCILE's *hands. Then, before she can hand it to him, he hurries away, just managing to dive behind the open door of Cécile's bedroom, as* VOLANGES *arrives.*)
VOLANGES: What are you doing?
(*Behind her,* VALMONT *tiptoes backwards across the opening between the two rooms. Meanwhile,* CÉCILE *gropes for an answer.*)
CÉCILE: I just came up to fetch your shawl.
(*She picks up* VOLANGES's *shawl from a chair and hands it to her, giving* VALMONT *the opportunity to make his escape across the anteroom.*)

INT. MAIN STAIRCASE. DAY
VOLANGES *follows* CÉCILE *down the staircase. All of a sudden* CÉCILE *stumbles in shock, allowing her mother to overtake her.*

What has caused her surprise is that VALMONT *has somehow arrived at the bottom of the stairs and is now approaching them. As he passes he fumbles discreetly at* CÉCILE's *hand, but nothing happens. He grimaces in extreme annoyance, but* CÉCILE *has been more alert than he imagined possible; and the key is sitting there, left by her on the stone banisters.* VALMONT *picks it up.*

EXT. FORMAL GARDENS. DAY
VALMONT *bears down on* TOURVEL *in a secluded corner of the rigidly manicured gardens. He perches on the end of the stone bench, where she's sitting.*
VALMONT: Why are you so angry with me?
TOURVEL: All I can offer you, monsieur, is my friendship; can't you accept it?
VALMONT: I could pretend to; but that would be dishonest. The man I used to be would have been content with friendship; and set about trying to turn it to his advantage. But I've changed now; and I can't conceal from you that I love you tenderly, passionately . . .
   (TOURVEL *gets up and moves away agitatedly, causing* VALMONT *to change tack smoothly.*)
   . . . and, above all, respectfully. So how am I to demote myself to the tepid position of friend? Not that you've even been pretending to show friendship.
TOURVEL: What do you mean?
VALMONT: Well, is this friendly?
   (*And having worked himself up into a fine indignation,* VALMONT *begins to stride away, until, as he's calculated,* TOURVEL *stops him with her protest.*)
TOURVEL: Why must you deliberately destroy my peace of mind?
   (VALMONT *turns and walks back to her, finally speaking with the greatest earnestness.*)
VALMONT: You're wrong to feel threatened by me, madame. Your happiness is far more important to me than my own. That is what I mean when I say I love you.
TOURVEL: I think we should end this conversation.
VALMONT: I shall leave you in possession of the field.

33

(*He turns and walks away; then stops and addresses her again.*)
But look: we're to be living under the same roof at least for a few days. Surely we don't have to try to avoid each other?

TOURVEL: Of course not. Provided you adhere to my few simple rules.

VALMONT: I shall obey you in this as in everything.
(*Rather to her surprise, he bows formally and moves off.*)

TOURVEL: Monsieur?

VALMONT: What?
(*She looks at him for a moment, troubled; then shakes her head.*)

TOURVEL: Nothing.
(VALMONT *permits himself a private smile and disappears.* TOURVEL *stands, not moving, locked in some private struggle.*)

INT. ANTEROOM TO THE VOLANGES' BEDROOMS. NIGHT
The hinges no longer squeak as VALMONT, *in his dressing-gown, carrying a candlestick, closes the door behind him, produces the key, crosses to another door, inserts the key in the lock, turns it, removes and pockets the key, opens the door and advances.*

INT. CÉCILE'S BEDROOM. NIGHT
CÉCILE *is fast asleep in the large bed.* VALMONT *closes the door behind him and crosses silently to the bed. He stands for a moment, contemplating* CÉCILE. *Then he puts the candlestick down carefully, leans forward and very gently eases back the covers.* CÉCILE *stirs but still doesn't wake.* VALMONT *passes his hand through the air, tracing the contours of her body. Finally, he puts his hand over her mouth. She wakes with a start, her eyes wide above his hand.* VALMONT *smiles and speaks in a whisper.*

VALMONT: Nothing to worry about.
(*He removes his hand. She stares up at him, frowning.*)

CÉCILE: Have you brought a letter?

VALMONT: No.

CÉCILE: Then what . . .

(*Instead of answering, he leans forward to kiss her. There's a brief, fierce struggle, in which* CÉCILE *successfully defends herself from the kiss, but is entirely taken by surprise when* VALMONT *plunges a hand up inside her nightdress. Her eyes widen in horror, but her cry is instantly stifled as* VALMONT'*s other hand clamps down on her mouth. She writhes determinedly for a moment, succeeds in freeing her head and dives across the bed to reach for the bell-pull.* VALMONT *leaps on to the bed, grasping her wrist just in time. She grapples with him for a moment.*)

VALMONT: What are you going to tell your mother? How will you explain the fact that I have your key? If I tell her I'm here at your invitation, I have a feeling she'll believe me. (CÉCILE *stops struggling, her eyes wide with fear. He's lying beside her on the bed.*)

CÉCILE: What do you want?

VALMONT: Well, I don't know. What do you think?

(*His hand goes back up inside her nightdress.*)

CÉCILE: No!

VALMONT: All right. I just want you to give me a kiss.

CÉCILE: A kiss?

VALMONT: That's all.

CÉCILE: Then will you go?

VALMONT: Then I'll go.

CÉCILE: Promise?

VALMONT: Whatever you say.

(CÉCILE *flops back on the pillow and closes her eyes.*)

CÉCILE: All right.

(VALMONT *leans in and gives her a long kiss, his hands roaming as he does so. After a while he pulls away.*)

All right?

VALMONT: Very nice.

CÉCILE: No, I mean, will you go now?

VALMONT: Oh, I don't think so.

CÉCILE: But you promised.

VALMONT: I promised to go when you gave me a kiss. You didn't give me a kiss. I gave you a kiss. Not the same thing at all.

35

(CÉCILE *peers at him miserably. He looks back at her,*
calmly waiting.)
CÉCILE: And if I give you a kiss . . . ?
VALMONT: Let's just get ourselves more comfortable, shall
we?
(*He leans over to reach the sheet and dispose it over them, as*
CÉCILE *stares at him, transfixed.*)

INT. DINING-ROOM. DAY
ROSEMONDE *sits at the head of the polished table, with* CÉCILE
on her right and VALMONT *on her left. Further down, on*
VALMONT's *side, is* VOLANGES; *opposite her,* TOURVEL. *It's*
breakfast time and the sideboard is groaning with beef and poultry
and lamb cutlets. VALMONT *is eating heartily;* CÉCILE, *on the*
other hand, stares unseeingly at the proffered plate of cutlets. She
looks up. Across the table, VALMONT *catches her eye and leers at*
her. As her distress mounts, he makes another unmistakably
lascivious moue. *Immediately, she bursts into noisy tears, gets up*
and hurries out of the room. Consternation, except for VALMONT,
who, unperturbed, sips at his champagne.
VOLANGES: I'd better go and see what's wrong, if you'll
excuse me.
ROSEMONDE: Of course, my dear.
VALMONT: I shouldn't worry, madame. The young have such
miraculous powers of recuperation. I'm sure she'll soon
be back in the saddle.
(VOLANGES, *on her feet already, acknowledges* VALMONT
with a perfunctory smile, as she hurries out of the room. He
catches TOURVEL's *eye and smiles at her, as she looks back*
at him, bemused.)

INT. ANTEROOM. NIGHT
VALMONT *tiptoes in, carrying a candlestick. He reaches Cécile's*
door, brings out his key and turns it in the lock. The door does not
yield. VALMONT *frowns, puzzled, and tries again.*

INT. CÉCILE'S BEDROOM. NIGHT
The door is bolted on the inside. CÉCILE *sits at her bureau,*

36

writing a letter, tears rolling down her face. She looks up at the
sound of the key in the lock, then returns with an even fiercer
concentration to her letter.
CÉCILE: (*Voice over*) 'Who else can I turn to in my desperation,
madame?'

INT. DRESSING-ROOM IN MERTEUIL'S HOUSE. DAY
MERTEUIL *reads, her face concealed by Cécile's letter.*
CÉCILE: (*Voice over*) 'And how can I write the necessary
words?'
(MERTEUIL *lowers the letter to reveal a smile of sardonic
relish.*)

EXT. MAIN ENTRANCE TO ROSEMONDE'S CHATEAU. DAY
*A large and elegant carriage draws up outside the château. The
head footman, a silver-haired veteran, passes down the steps
through the ranks of servants, who wait at attention, opens the
carriage door, lowers the steps and remains bowed in anticipation.
Presently the* MARQUISE DE MERTEUIL *emerges from the
carriage.*
VOLANGES *hurries down the steps between the ranks of servants
and mutters urgently to* MERTEUIL *as they embrace.*
VOLANGES: There's something going on, Cécile won't tell me,
you must speak to her at once.

INT. DRAWING-ROOM IN THE CHATEAU. DAY
CÉCILE *kneels at* MERTEUIL'*s feet.*
MERTEUIL: Tell me: you resisted him, did you?
CÉCILE: Of course I did, as much as I could.
MERTEUIL: But he forced you?
CÉCILE: No: not exactly, but I found it almost impossible to
defend myself.
MERTEUIL: Why was that? Did he tie you up?
CÉCILE: No. No, but he has a way of putting things. You just
can't think of an answer.
MERTEUIL: Not even 'no'?
CÉCILE: I kept saying no all the time; but somehow that
wasn't what I was doing.

(*She looks up at* MERTEUIL.)

I'm so ashamed.

MERTEUIL: You'll find the shame is like the pain.

(*She's on her feet now, crossing to the mirror, in front of which she removes her hat; and adds with a sudden melancholy.*)

You only feel it once.

(*She sits down again, turning back to* CÉCILE.)

You really want my advice?

(CÉCILE *gets up and goes over to sit next to her on the sofa.*)

Allow Monsieur de Valmont to continue your instruction. Convince your mother you have forgotten Danceny. And raise no objection to the marriage.

(CÉCILE *gapes at her, bewildered.*)

CÉCILE: With Monsieur de Bastide?

MERTEUIL: When it comes to marriage one man is as good as the next; and even the least accommodating is less trouble than a mother.

CÉCILE: Are you saying I'm going to have to do that with three different men?

MERTEUIL: I'm saying, you stupid little girl, that provided you take a few elementary precautions, you can do it, or not, with as many men as you like, as often as you like, in as many different ways as you like. Our sex has few enough advantages, you may as well make the most of those you have.

(CÉCILE *is fascinated: she looks at* MERTEUIL *with a kind of wild surmise.*)

And now here comes your mama, so remember what I've said and, above all, no snivelling.

(VOLANGES *arrives from the next room, anxiously looking at* CÉCILE.)

VOLANGES: How are you feeling now, my dear?

CÉCILE: Oh, much better, thank you, maman.

VOLANGES: You look so tired. I think you should to to bed.

CÉCILE: No, really, I . . .

MERTEUIL: I think you should do as your mother suggests. We can arrange for something to be brought to your room. I'm sure it would do you good.

CÉCILE: Well. Perhaps you're right, madame.
(And she leaves the room, turning back once to exchange a mischievous glance with MERTEUIL. VOLANGES *doesn't see this, having turned gratefully back to* MERTEUIL.)
VOLANGES: You have such a very good influence on her.

INT. GRAND SALON. EVENING
ROSEMONDE *is entertaining members of the local nobility and everyone has made an effort to do justice to the occasion.*
VALMONT *and* MERTEUIL *move through the crowd, resplendent, conversing in an undertone, as they acknowledge the greetings of their acquaintances.* VALMONT *makes a particularly deep reverence to* VOLANGES *and* CÉCILE, *at which the former smiles in queasy response.* VALMONT *kisses* CÉCILE's *hand before she moves off with her mother.*
MERTEUIL: I don't think I've congratulated you on your revenge.
VALMONT: So you know.
MERTEUIL: Oh yes. And I believe from now on you'll find her door unbolted.
(VALMONT is not best pleased by this. MERTEUIL has moved away and he sets off after her.)
Where is she?
VALMONT: Can't see her at the moment. Surely I've explained to you before how much I enjoy watching the battle between love and virtue.
MERTEUIL: What concerns me is that you appear to enjoy watching it more than you used to enjoy winning it.
VALMONT: All in good time.
MERTEUIL: The century is drawing to its close.
(Their travels have brought them back close to VOLANGES *and* CÉCILE, *whom* VALMONT *surreptitiously indicates.)*
VALMONT: Isn't it a pity that our agreement does not relate to the task you set me rather than the task I set myself?
MERTEUIL: I am grateful, of course: but that would have been almost insultingly simple. One does not applaud the tenor for clearing his throat.
(As VALMONT *smiles at this sally, there begins the orchestral*

39

introduction to the aria 'Ombra mai fù' from Handel's
Xerxes.)

INT. GRAND SALON. NIGHT
As the music continues, TOURVEL *makes her way into the grand
salon, where she arrives as the aria begins.*
*The aria is sung in a pure and unearthly soprano by a man of
melancholy aspect: a castrato. He stands on a dais in front of a
small baroque orchestra, singing exquisitely, the veins standing out
on his temples.*
TOURVEL *pauses in the doorway. Among the audience are*
VALMONT *and* MERTEUIL, CÉCILE, ROSEMONDE *and*
VOLANGES, *the latter somewhat bemused by the castrato.*
As he continues, TOURVEL, *looking frail and exhausted, pauses
again behind* MERTEUIL *and* VALMONT. VALMONT *watches her
make her way along the row to an empty seat.* MERTEUIL *notices
his preoccupation and follows his eyeline. Then she looks away.*
TOURVEL *reaches her seat and sits. Along the row,* VALMONT *is
watching her, transfixed.*
MERTEUIL *turns back and becomes aware that* VALMONT *is in
another world. She frowns, disturbed.*
TOURVEL *turns to look at* VALMONT.
At the other end of the row, VALMONT *continues to stare gravely
at* TOURVEL; *while* MERTEUIL *quickly looks away.*
TOURVEL *smiles shyly at* VALMONT.
VALMONT *turns away sheepishly and kisses* MERTEUIL's *hand.*
TOURVEL *can't resist looking at* VALMONT *again.*
And VALMONT *returns her gaze uneasily, as the aria comes to a
close.*

INT. UPSTAIRS CORRIDOR. NIGHT
VALMONT, *carrying a candlestick, leads* CÉCILE *along the
corridor. They're both in dressing-gowns. Below, a servant
ascends the stairs.* VALMONT *and* CÉCILE *hurry away.*

INT. VALMONT'S BEDROOM. NIGHT
VALMONT *stands at the foot of the bed, taking off his slippers, as*
CÉCILE *tugs at his shirt.*

VALMONT: As with every other science, the first thing you must learn is to call everything by its proper name.

CÉCILE: I don't see why you have to talk at all.

VALMONT: Without the correct polite vocabulary, how can you indicate what you would like me to do or make me an offer of something I might find agreeable?

CÉCILE: Surely you just . . . ?

(*Impulsively,* CÉCILE *is pulling off her nightdress;* VALMONT *leans over to help her.*)

VALMONT: You see, if I do my work adequately, I would like to think you'll be able to surprise Monsieur de Bastide on his wedding night.

CÉCILE: Would he be pleased?

(*His task completed,* VALMONT *lowers himself on to the bed with her.*)

VALMONT: Of course, he'll merely assume your mama has done her duty and fully briefed you.

CÉCILE: Maman couldn't possibly talk about anything of the sort.

VALMONT: I can't think why. She was, after all, at one time, one of the most notorious young women in Paris.

CÉCILE: Maman?

VALMONT: Certainly. More noted for her enthusiasm than her ability, if I remember rightly. There was a famous occasion, oh, before you were born, this would have been, when she went to stay with the Comtesse de Beaulieu, who tactfully gave her a room between your father's and that of a Monsieur de Vressac, who was her acknowledged lover at the time. Yet in spite of these careful arrangements, she contrived to spend the night with a third party.

CÉCILE: I can't believe that.

VALMONT: No, no, I assure you, it's true.

CÉCILE: How do you know?

(VALMONT *looks down at her, a slow smile spreading.*)

VALMONT: The third party was myself.

(CÉCILE's *jaw drops. For a moment she stares at* VALMONT, *appalled. Then she bursts out laughing, her laughter*

41

abandoned. *He lets her finish, then closes her mouth with a kiss.*)
You asked me if Monsieur de Bastide would be pleased with your abilities; and the answer is: education is never a waste.
(*He caresses her thoughtfully, and begins kissing her, his head travelling down her body. He plants a kiss on her stomach and looks up at her.*)
Now, I think we might begin with one or two Latin terms.

INT. PRIVATE CHAPEL. DAY
The Curé is intoning the mass, when VALMONT *arrives, late. He genuflects, pleased to notice that the seat next to* TOURVEL *is empty, possibly even reserved for him by her. He sits, yawning and winking at* CÉCILE. TOURVEL *looks up at him, welcoming.*

EXT. GROUNDS OF THE CHATEAU. DAY
VALMONT *and* TOURVEL *stroll through parklands, the château silhouetted on a ridge behind them, deep in conversation.*
VALMONT: (*Voice over*) 'We go for a walk together almost every day: a little further every time down the path that has no turning.'

INT. DRESSING-ROOM IN MERTEUIL'S HOUSE. DAY
MERTEUIL *sits, in her* négligé, *reading a letter.*
VALMONT: (*Voice over*) 'She's accepted my love; I've accepted her friendship.'

EXT. GROUNDS OF THE CHATEAU. DAY
VALMONT *and* TOURVEL *continue to approach.*
VALMONT: (*Voice over*) 'We're both aware how little there is to choose between them.'
(*They arrive within earshot.*)
I wish you knew me well enough to recognize how much you've changed me. My friends in Paris remarked on it at once. I've become the soul of consideration, charitable, conscientious, more celibate than a monk . . .

TOURVEL: More celibate?
VALMONT: Well, you know the stories one hears in
    Paris.
    (TOURVEL *can't suppress a smile. Long shot: the two of*
    them moving through the autumn landscape.)
    (*Voice over*) 'I feel sure that she is inches from surrender.'

INT. MERTEUIL'S DRESSING-ROOM. DAY
MERTEUIL *continues to read.*
VALMONT: (*Voice over*) 'Her eyes are closing.'
(*She looks up, thoughtful.*)

INT. VALMONT'S BEDROOM. NIGHT
VALMONT *stands, still fully dressed, in his candlelit bedroom, his*
door slightly ajar, his eye to the crack in the door. A peal of
thunder in the distance.

INT. CORRIDOR. NIGHT
VALMONT'*s point of view through the crack in the door;*
TOURVEL, *alone, arrives at the top of the stairs.*

INT. VALMONT'S BEDROOM. NIGHT
VALMONT *straightens up and saunters out of his room.*

INT. CORRIDOR. NIGHT
VALMONT *stops, as if surprised, and bows to* TOURVEL.
VALMONT: Madame.
TOURVEL: Where are you going, monsieur?
VALMONT: To the salon.
TOURVEL: There's no one there. The others have all decided
    on an early night.
    (*He's following her along the corridor now, on the way to her*
    room.)
VALMONT: I very much missed our walk today.
TOURVEL: Yes.
VALMONT: I fear with the weather as it is, we can look
    forward to very few more of them.
TOURVEL: This heavy rain is surely exceptional.

VALMONT: Oh, yes.

(*By this time, they've arrived at the door to her bedroom, which she's opened. She hesitates in the doorway and* VALMONT *decides to take a chance.*)

May I?

TOURVEL: Of course.

(*Trying to conceal his astonishment, he follows her into the room.*)

INT. TOURVEL'S BEDROOM. NIGHT

VALMONT *speaks, to cover his entrance into the room, which is similarly appointed to his own, though somehow far more sober in feeling.*

VALMONT: But, you see, within a week I shall have concluded my business.

(TOURVEL *stops in her tracks, clearly affected by this news.*)

TOURVEL: I see.

VALMONT: Even so, I'm not sure I'll be able to bring myself to leave.

TOURVEL: Oh, please. You must!

(*It's an involuntary exclamation;* VALMONT *knows exactly how to capitalize on it.*)

VALMONT: Are you still so anxious to be rid of me?

TOURVEL: You know the answer to that. I rely on your integrity and generosity. I want to be able to be grateful to you.

VALMONT: Forgive me if I say I don't want your gratitude. What I want from you is something altogether deeper.

(*She turns and begins to move away from him.*)

TOURVEL: I know God is punishing me for my pride. I was so certain nothing like this could ever happen.

VALMONT: Nothing like what?

TOURVEL: I can't . . .

VALMONT: Do you mean love? Is love what you mean?

(*He's pursued her and now they begin to circle one another as she tries to escape and the words come tumbling out.*)

TOURVEL: You promised not to speak of it.

VALMONT: Yes, of course, I understand, but I must know, I must know if . . .

44

TOURVEL: I can't . . . don't you understand . . . it's
impossible . . .
VALMONT: . . . if you love me, you don't have to speak, you
don't have to speak, just look at me.
(*Long silence. Finally, slowly,* TOURVEL *raises her eyes to
him.*)
TOURVEL: Yes.
(*They're motionless for a moment. Then* VALMONT *releases
her hand and puts his arms around her. As he does so, her
eyes suddenly go dead and she collapses sideways, obliging
him to catch her. She sways in his arms for a moment, then
comes to and jerks violently away from him, running halfway
across the room. Then she bursts into tears. She stands for a
moment, sobbing wildly, then rushes at* VALMONT, *falls to
her knees and throws her arms round his legs.*)
For God's sake, you must leave me, if you don't want to
kill me. You must help!
(VALMONT, *somewhat taken aback at first by her intensity,
collects himself and lifts her to her feet. For a moment, they
sway together in an ungainly embrace; then* TOURVEL's *sobs
cease abruptly and give way to chattering teeth and almost
epileptic convulsions. Startled,* VALMONT *gathers her up in
his arms, carries her over and deposits her gently on the bed.
The convulsions continue, her teeth are clenched, the blood
drained from her face. He leans forward and loosens her bodice
as she stares helplessly up at him. Slowly, her features return to
normal. He looks down at her, perplexed. Her arms open, she
relaxes, her lips part. He starts to lean towards her, then
suddenly checks himself and looks away, something almost like
shame darkening his expression. Her face begins to collapse. He
looks back at her, gnawing at his lip. She begins to go into shock
again and he straightens up. Her sobs drive him from the room.*)

INT. CORRIDOR. NIGHT
As VALMONT *steps into the corridor,* ROSEMONDE's *maid,*
ADELE, *comes hurrying up, struggling into her dressing-gown.*
VALMONT: Fetch madame. Madame de Tourvel has been
taken ill.

45

(ADELE *hurries away and* VALMONT *steels himself to step back into the room.*)

INT. TOURVEL'S BEDROOM. NIGHT
As VALMONT *appears in the doorway,* TOURVEL *stretches out her hand to him. He crosses and takes it between both of his. He stands, massaging her hand, bemused and thoughtful. He lets go of her hand abruptly as* ROSEMONDE *appears, shepherded by* ADELE.
VALMONT: I heard something as I was passing; she seemed to be having difficulty breathing.
ROSEMONDE: Oh, my dear, whatever is it?
TOURVEL: I'm all right now.
VALMONT: I shall leave her in your capable hands, Aunt.
　(*And still looking strangely abashed, he leaves the room.*)
ROSEMONDE: We must send for a doctor, my dear.
　(TOURVEL *is roused from her rapt contemplation of* VALMONT's *departure.*)
TOURVEL: No, no, please, I don't need a doctor. I just . . . sit with me for a moment.

INT. CORRIDOR. NIGHT
VOLANGES *hurries down the corridor, on her way to investigate the disturbance. She's blocked by* VALMONT, *who grimaces at her, uttering a bizarre hiss to discourage her from entering* TOURVEL's *room. She hesitates, then turns away, strangely unnerved. As she recedes,* VALMONT *looks again at* TOURVEL's *door, then moves away and sinks on to a bench in the long corridor, completely mystified.*

INT. TOURVEL'S BEDROOM. NIGHT
ADELE *finishes lighting the candles and leaves the room.*
ROSEMONDE's *kindly face looks anxiously down at* TOURVEL. *They're holding hands.* TOURVEL *speaks very quietly, controlling herself with enormous difficulty.*
TOURVEL: I must leave this house. I'm most desperately in love.
　(ROSEMONDE *bows her head, unsurprised.*)

46

To leave is the last thing in the world I want to do, but I'd rather die than have to live with the guilt.

ROSEMONDE: My dear girl. None of this is any surprise to me. The only thing which might surprise one is how little the world changes.

TOURVEL: Well, what should I do? What's your advice?

ROSEMONDE: If I remember rightly, in such matters all advice is useless.

TOURVEL: I've never been so unhappy.

ROSEMONDE: I'm sorry to say this: but those who are most worthy of love are never made happy by it.

TOURVEL: But why, why should that be?

ROSEMONDE: Do you still think men love the way we do? No. Men enjoy the happiness they feel; we can only enjoy the happiness we give. They're not capable of devoting themselves exclusively to one person. So to hope to be made happy by love is a certain cause of grief. I'm devoted to my nephew, but what's true of most men is doubly so of him.

TOURVEL: And yet . . . he could have . . . just now. He took pity on me.

ROSEMONDE: If he has released you, my dear child, you must go.

(TOURVEL *looks up at her. Tears begin to cascade from the corners of her eyes.*)

INT. VALMONT'S BEDROOM. NIGHT

AZOLAN *leans over* VALMONT, *shaking him.* VALMONT *comes up from the bottom of a deep sleep and wakes with a start.*

AZOLAN: Get up, sir, quick.

VALMONT: What is it?

(AZOLAN *is already over by the window.*)

AZOLAN: Over here.

(VALMONT, *spurred by the urgency of his tone, scrambles out of bed and joins him at the window.*)

VALMONT: What is it?

AZOLAN: Madame de Tourvel.

(*Suddenly,* VALMONT *is wide awake.*)

VALMONT: What?

INT. MAIN ENTRANCE. NIGHT
Below, a carriage pulls away and speeds down the entrance drive.

INT. VALMONT'S BEDROOM. NIGHT
VALMONT *issues his orders calmly and decisively.*
VALMONT: I want you to follow her, right now. Stay close to
her. I want to know everything. Who she sees, where she
goes, what she eats, if she sleeps. Everything.
*(He's fetched what looks like a great deal of money out of his
desk. He throws it across the room to AZOLAN.)*
That's for bribes. Yours will come later.
AZOLAN: Yes, sir.
VALMONT: Now go. Go!
*(AZOLAN hurries out of the room. VALMONT looks back
towards the window, the shock beginning to show.)*

INT. TOURVEL'S DRAWING-ROOM. DAY
TOURVEL *sits at her desk, writing a letter.*
TOURVEL: *(Voice over)* 'Dear Father Anselme: try as I may I
cannot see the necessity for the interview you suggest.
However, since you insist, I propose you bring him to see
me on Tuesday the 28th at six o'clock p.m.'
(JULIE passes by in the background.)

INT. DRAWING-ROOM IN VALMONT'S HOUSE. DAY
VALMONT *is reading the letter. Presently, he hands it to*
AZOLAN, *who is standing nearby with a self-satisfied expression.*
VALMONT: This is excellent. Make sure Father Anselme
receives it. What news?
(He settles himself at his desk.)
AZOLAN: No visitors. There still hasn't been a single visitor
since she got back.

INT. DRAWING-ROOM IN TOURVEL'S HOUSE. NIGHT
TOURVEL *sits staring sightlessly into space; beside her, a tray
of food, scarcely disturbed. There are dark circles under her
eyes.*

48

AZOLAN: (*Voice over*) Bit of soup last night but didn't touch the pheasant. Afterwards a cup of tea. Nothing else to report. Oh yes, there is. You wanted to know what she was reading.

INT. DRAWING-ROOM IN VALMONT'S HOUSE. DAY
AZOLAN *smiles complacently.*
AZOLAN: The book by her bed is *Christian Thoughts: Volume Two*.
(VALMONT, *pleased, hands* AZOLAN *some gold coins.*)
VALMONT: How's Julie?
AZOLAN: Seems a bit keener than she was in the country.
VALMONT: And yourself?
(AZOLAN *sighs, shaking his head gloomily.*)
AZOLAN: Talk about devotion to duty.
(MERTEUIL *and* DANCENY *are shown into the room.*
VALMONT *dismisses* AZOLAN, *speaking out of the side of his mouth.*)
VALMONT: Off you go. Keep it up.
(VALMONT *kisses* MERTEUIL's *hand, as* AZOLAN *leaves the room.*)
Madame.
MERTEUIL: Vicomte.
(*She turns, making him aware of* DANCENY.)
VALMONT: Well!
(*He exchanges a pregnant glance with* MERTEUIL, *before crossing to* DANCENY.)
What a pleasant surprise!
(*He embraces him, kissing him on both cheeks.*)
Danceny!
DANCENY: Thank you, monsieur, for everything.
VALMONT: I was afraid I'd been a sad disappointment to you.
DANCENY: On the contrary, it's you I have to thank for keeping our love alive.
VALMONT: Ah, as to love, Cécile thinks of little else. She and her mother are coming back to Paris in two weeks and she's longing to see you.
DANCENY: I've had the most wonderful letter from her.

49

VALMONT: Really?

DANCENY: Not like any of her other letters. Somehow quite a different tone of voice.

(MERTEUIL, *watching in the mirror, has to disguise her laughter with a cough*.)

CÉCILE: (*Voice over*) 'My dearest Danceny . . .'

INT. VALMONT'S BEDROOM IN ROSEMONDE'S CHATEAU.
NIGHT

CÉCILE *is taking dictation from* VALMONT, *pressing on his bare back*.

CÉCILE: '. . . I swear to you . . .'

VALMONT: '. . . on my chastity, that even if my mother forces me to go through with this marriage, comma, I shall be yours completely. Your friend, the Vicomte de Valmont . . .'

INT. GRAND SALON IN MERTEUIL'S HOUSE. DAY

MERTEUIL *is reading the finished letter*.

VALMONT: (*Voice over*) '. . . has been very active on your behalf. I doubt if you could do more yourself.'

(MERTEUIL *smiles, folding up the letter*.)

INT. DRAWING-ROOM IN VALMONT'S HOUSE. DAY

DANCENY: I don't know how I can bear to go another two weeks without seeing her.

MERTEUIL: We shall have to do our very best to provide some distraction for you. And now, if you'd be so kind as to wait in the carriage, there's a matter I must discuss with the Vicomte in private.

DANCENY: Of course.

(*He bows to* VALMONT *and pumps his hand heartily*.)

I don't know how I can ever repay you.

VALMONT: Don't give it another thought, it's been delightful.

(DANCENY *leaves the room and* VALMONT *and* MERTEUIL *look at one another*.)

Poor boy. He's quite harmless.

MERTEUIL: Sometimes, Vicomte, I can't help but adore you.

VALMONT: I have a piece of news I hope you might find entertaining: I have reason to believe the next head of the house of Bastide may be a Valmont.

MERTEUIL: What can you mean?

VALMONT: Cécile is two weeks late.

(MERTEUIL *is startled; she frowns, assessing the implications.*)

Aren't you pleased?

MERTEUIL: I'm not sure.

VALMONT: Your aim was to revenge yourself on Bastide. I've provided him with a wife trained by me to perform quite naturally services you would hesitate to request from a professional and very likely pregnant as well. What more do you want?

MERTEUIL: All right, Vicomte, I agree, you've more than done your duty. Shame you let the other one slip through your fingers.

(VALMONT'*s expression darkens.*)

VALMONT: I let her go.

MERTEUIL: But why?

VALMONT: I was . . . moved.

MERTEUIL: Oh, well, then, no wonder you bungled it.

VALMONT: I have an appointment to visit her on Thursday. And this time, I shall be merciless.

MERTEUIL: I'm pleased to hear it.

VALMONT: Why do you suppose we only feel compelled to chase the ones who run away?

MERTEUIL: Immaturity?

VALMONT: I shan't have a moment's peace until it's over, you know. I love her, I hate her, my life's a misery.

(MERTEUIL, *not best pleased by this, pretends to suppress a yawn.*)

MERTEUIL: I think I may have kept our young friend waiting long enough.

VALMONT: I shall call on you sometime soon after Thursday.

MERTEUIL: Only if you succeed, Vicomte. I'm not sure I could face another catalogue of incompetence.

VALMONT: I shall succeed.

MERTEUIL: I hope so: once upon a time, you were a man to be reckoned with.

(*She hurries away, leaving* VALMONT *alone and troubled.*)

INT. ENTRANCE HALL IN TOURVEL'S HOUSE. EVENING
Tourvel's footman, GEORGES, *and* FATHER ANSELME, *by appearance an amiably dim-witted Cistercian, beckon* VALMONT *in. Outside the drawing-room,* VALMONT *murmurs in* FATHER ANSELME'*s ear and the latter, after a moment's hesitation, sits down in the hall.* VALMONT *drops to one knee, kisses* FATHER ANSELME'*s hand and steps into the room.*

INT. DRAWING-ROOM IN TOURVEL'S HOUSE. EVENING
TOURVEL *is sitting with her back to the door. As* VALMONT *follows* GEORGES *into the room, she struggles to her feet, visibly trembling, ethereal with exhaustion.* GEORGES *is surprised to be dismissed impatiently with a gesture from* TOURVEL.

VALMONT: I understand Father Anselme has explained to you the reasons for my visit.

TOURVEL: Yes. He said you wished to be reconciled with me before beginning instruction with him.

VALMONT: That's correct.

TOURVEL: But I see no need for formal reconciliation, monsieur.

VALMONT: No? When I have, as you said, insulted you; and when you have treated me with unqualified contempt.

TOURVEL: Contempt?

VALMONT: You run away from my aunt's house in the middle of the night; you refuse to answer or even receive my letters: and all this after I have shown a restraint of which I think we are both aware. I would call that, at the very least, contempt.

TOURVEL: I'm sure you understand me better than you pretend, monsieur . . .

VALMONT: It was me you ran away from, wasn't it?

TOURVEL: I had to leave.

VALMONT: And do you have to keep away from me?

(TOURVEL *nods miserably.* VALMONT *moves away from her, speaking half to himself, it seems.*)
I'm as unhappy as you could ever have wanted me to be.
TOURVEL: I've only ever wanted your happiness.
VALMONT: How can I be happy without you?
(*He runs across to her, falling to his knees.*)
I must have you or die.
(*He buries his face in her lap. Cautiously, as if plunging it in boiling water,* TOURVEL *allows her hand to rest for a few seconds on* VALMONT's *head. Then she scrambles to her feet and retreats across the room.* VALMONT *remains on his knees.*)
Death it is.
(*She looks back at him, distraught. He rises to his feet, calmer now.*)
I'm sorry, madame. All I wanted from this meeting was your forgiveness for the wrongs you think I've done you, so that I may end my days in some peace of mind.
TOURVEL: I understood you approved of the choice my duty has compelled me to make.
VALMONT: Yes. And your choice has determined mine.
TOURVEL: Which is what?
VALMONT: The only choice capable of putting an end to my suffering.
(TOURVEL's *eyes are full of fear.*)
TOURVEL: What do you mean?
(VALMONT *puts his hands on her arms and almost shakes her.*)
VALMONT: Listen. I love you. You've no idea how much. Just remember I've made far more difficult sacrifices than the one I'm about to make. Now goodbye.
(*He pulls away from her, but she clutches at his wrist.*)
TOURVEL: No.
VALMONT: Let me go.
TOURVEL: You must listen to me!
VALMONT: I have to go.
TOURVEL: No!
(*During this exchange they have been struggling, he to free*

53

*himself, she to hang on to him. Now she collapses into his
arms and the struggle resolves into a long kiss. Then he
sweeps her up in his arms, carries her across the room and
gently sets her down on the ottoman. She bursts into tears
and clutches on to him as if she's drowning. Eventually he
speaks, his voice unusually tender.)*

VALMONT: Why should you be so upset by the idea of making
me happy?

(Gradually she stops crying, looking up at him.)

TOURVEL: Yes. You're right. I can't live either unless I make
you happy. So I promise. No more refusals and no more
regrets.

*(He leans in and kisses her gently. Then he looks at her for a
second and they begin tearing at one another's clothes,
suddenly both equally ravenous.)*

INT. MAIN STAIRCASE AND LANDING IN MERTEUIL'S
HOUSE. DAY

VALMONT *springs up the staircase, easily outpacing the puffing*
MAJORDOMO.

VALMONT: Success! Success!

INT. GRAND SALON IN MERTEUIL'S HOUSE. DAY

MERTEUIL *is looking up with eager anticipation.*

VALMONT: I arrived about six.

MERTEUIL: Yes, I think you may omit the details of the
seduction, they're never very enlivening: just describe the
event itself.

VALMONT: It was . . . unprecedented.

MERTEUIL: Really?

VALMONT: It had a kind of charm I don't think I've ever
experienced before.

*(MERTEUIL's facing away from him now, so he's unable to see
– or discern from her voice, which remains icy – that for her,
every word is like a dagger.)*

Once she'd surrendered, she behaved with perfect
candour. Total mutual delirium. Which for the first
time ever with me outlasted the pleasure itself. She was

54

astonishing. So much so that I ended by falling on my knees and pledging her eternal love.

INT. DRAWING-ROOM IN TOURVEL'S HOUSE. EVENING
VALMONT *and* TOURVEL, *their faces close, their expressions rapturous.*
VALMONT: (*Voice over*) And do you know, at the time . . .

INT. GRAND SALON IN MERTEUIL'S HOUSE. DAY
Close on VALMONT, *as he realizes he's allowed himself, perhaps unwisely, to be carried away.*
VALMONT: . . . and for several hours afterwards, I actually meant it.
MERTEUIL: I see.
VALMONT: It's extraordinary, isn't it?
MERTEUIL: Is it? It sounds to me perfectly commonplace.
VALMONT: No, no, I assure you. But of course the best thing about it is that I am now in a position to be able to claim my reward.
(*Hooking his foot under her chair, he begins to draw it towards him; but she rises abruptly and moves away across the room, digesting all that's been said, her expression grim.*)
MERTEUIL: You mean to say you persuaded her to write a letter as well, in the course of this awesome encounter?
VALMONT: I didn't necessarily think you were going to be a stickler for formalities.
MERTEUIL: In any case, I may have to declare our arrangement null and void.
(VALMONT *gets up, puzzled by her sudden vehemence.*)
VALMONT: What do you mean?
MERTEUIL: I'm not accustomed to being taken for granted.
VALMONT: But there's no question of that. You're misunderstanding me.
MERTEUIL: And I've no wish to tear you away from the arms of someone so astonishing.
VALMONT: We've always been frank with one another.
MERTEUIL: And as a matter of fact, I have also taken a new lover, who, at the moment, is proving more than satisfactory.

55

VALMONT: Oh? And who is that?

MERTEUIL: I am not in the mood for confidences. Don't let me keep you.

(*She turns and moves decisively away from a startled* VALMONT.)

INT. CORRIDOR OF MIRRORS. DAY

VALMONT *follows* MERTEUIL, *as she moves briskly along the corridor.*

VALMONT: You can't seriously imagine I prefer her to you?

MERTEUIL: You may genuinely be unaware of this. But I can see quite plainly that you're in love with this woman.

(VALMONT *stops in his tracks, shocked by the suggestion.*)

VALMONT: No.

(MERTEUIL *turns back to him.*)

Not at all.

MERTEUIL: Have you forgotten what it's like to make a woman happy: and to be made happy yourself?

VALMONT: I . . . of course not.

MERTEUIL: We loved each other once, didn't we? I think it was love. And you made me very happy.

VALMONT: And I could again. We just untied the knot, it was never broken.

MERTEUIL: Illusions, of course, are by their nature sweet.

VALMONT: I have no illusions. I lost them on my travels. Now I want to come home.

(*He's reached her side now, and leans in to kiss her cheek tenderly. She softens, her eyes closing.* VALMONT *straightens, his habitual expression back in place.*)

As for this present infatuation, it won't last. But, for the moment, it's beyond my control.

(MERTEUIL'*s smile vanishes; she moves away from him and he leaves the corridor, shrugging off her obvious displeasure.* MERTEUIL *moves slowly along the corridor; then she hesitates and turns back, her preoccupied stance reflected and distorted in the mirrors. Then, purposefully, she opens the secret door.*)

INT. SPIRAL STAIRCASE. DAY
At the top of the stairs, MERTEUIL *leans her forehead against
the wall, collecting herself.*

INT. MERTEUIL'S BEDROOM. DAY
Her smile now dazzling, MERTEUIL *steps into the room and
hurries over to an unidentified man.*

EXT. STREET. EVENING
A large carriage passes, MERTEUIL*'s pale face at the window.
There's someone next to her in the shadows, unrecognizable.*
MERTEUIL: (*Voice over*) 'My dear Vicomte: I'm obliged to go
    away for a couple of weeks, but I'm well aware of our
    arrangement.'

INT. VALMONT'S BEDROOM. DAY
VALMONT *lies in bed, re-reading the letter, a half-smile on his
face.*
MERTEUIL: (*Voice over*) 'On my return you and I will spend a
    single night together. We shall enjoy it enough to regret
    that it's to be our last; but then we shall remember that
    regret is an essential component of happiness. All this, of
    course, providing you are able to procure this famous
    letter.'

INT. VALMONT'S DRAWING-ROOM. NIGHT
VALMONT *sits at his desk, writing.*
VALMONT: (*Voice over*) 'It shall be done . . .'

INT. BEDROOM IN MERTEUIL'S SUBURBAN VILLA.
EVENING
MERTEUIL, *in her négligé, sits reading the letter. In the
background, face down in the bed, a man stirs in his sleep.*
VALMONT: (*Voice over*) '. . . but Paris is so tedious without
    you; and I am living like a medieval hermit.'

INT. VALMONT'S DRAWING-ROOM. DAY
VALMONT *is deep in an embrace with* ÉMILIE, *when* AZOLAN

57

arrives and murmurs in his ear. Whatever he says seems to be an unpleasant surprise to VALMONT.

VALMONT: All right, give me a moment.

(*He turns back to* ÉMILIE *as* AZOLAN *leaves, indicating her champagne glass.*)

Drink up.

ÉMILIE: What is it?

VALMONT: Someone who may well not appreciate your presence.

ÉMILIE: You mean a woman?

VALMONT: A lady, we might even say.

ÉMILIE: Oh, not the one we wrote that letter to?

VALMONT: The very one.

ÉMILIE: I enjoyed that.

VALMONT: And you proved a most talented desk.

ÉMILIE: I'd love to see what she looks like.

VALMONT: Well, you can't.

(VALMONT *is having some difficulty disentangling himself from* ÉMILIE. *Finally he tears himself away and draws her to her feet. Suddenly, there is a strange, reckless excitement in his eyes.*)

On second thoughts, I don't see why you shouldn't.

INT. ENTRANCE HALL. DAY

AZOLAN *receives* TOURVEL *and sets off, moving very slowly, towards the drawing-room.*

INT. VALMONT'S DRAWING-ROOM. DAY

VALMONT *still can't tear himself away from* ÉMILIE.

VALMONT: Tell me: do you have plans for this evening?

ÉMILIE: A few friends for dinner.

VALMONT: And after dinner?

ÉMILIE: Nothing firm.

(*He moves away at last, heading for his desk.*)

VALMONT: Well . . .

INT. DOWNSTAIRS CORRIDOR. DAY

To AZOLAN'*s alarm,* TOURVEL *manages, in her eagerness, to overtake him.*

INT. VALMONT'S DRAWING-ROOM. DAY
TOURVEL *hurries into the room and stops in her tracks, startled.*
Her point of view: VALMONT *is handing* ÉMILIE *some money.*
This done, he kisses her on both cheeks. She looks at TOURVEL, *a*
sardonic smile on her face. VALMONT *watches, plainly enjoying*
himself.
TOURVEL *lowers her eyes, miserably confused.*
ÉMILIE: I'll be there.
    (*She walks towards* TOURVEL, *staring at her with un-*
    disguised fascination. At the last minute, just as she's
    leaving, ÉMILIE *is suddenly convulsed with mirth. She*
    vanishes, shaking with laughter, and AZOLAN *withdraws,*
    closing the double doors behind him.)
VALMONT: This is an unexpected pleasure.
TOURVEL: I know that woman.
VALMONT: Are you sure? I'd be surprised.
TOURVEL: She's been pointed out to me at the Opéra.
VALMONT: Yes, well, she is striking.
TOURVEL: She's a courtesan. Isn't she?
VALMONT: I suppose, in a manner of speaking . . .
    (*He's moved over to cut off her exit: just in time, for she now*
    makes a decisive effort to leave the room. He takes hold of
    her shoulders to block her and she struggles with him as her
    anger rises.)
TOURVEL: I'm sorry to have disturbed you.
VALMONT: Of course you haven't disturbed me, I'm overjoyed
    to see you.
TOURVEL: Please let me go now.
VALMONT: No, no, I can't, this is absurd.
TOURVEL: And you will never be received at my house again!
VALMONT: Let's sit down . . .
TOURVEL: I don't want your lies and excuses!
VALMONT: Just hear me out, that's all I ask. Then you can
    judge.
    (*He locks the door behind him and lets the key drop on to the*
    floor. Then he forces her over to a sofa and sits her down. He
    settles himself on a nearby stool and begins to speak with
    unruffled calm. She watches him, transfixed.)

Unfortunately, I cannot unlive the years I lived before I met you, and during those years I had a wide acquaintance, the majority of whom were no doubt undesirable in one respect or another. Now, it may surprise you to know that Émilie, in common with many others of her profession and character, is kind-hearted enough to take an interest in those less fortunate than herself. She has, in short, the free time and the inclination to do a great deal of charity work: donations to hospitals, soup for the poor, protection for animals, anything which touches her sentimental heart. From time to time, I make small contributions to her purse. That's all.

TOURVEL: Is that true?

VALMONT: My relations with Émilie have for some years now been quite blameless. She's even done a little secretarial work for me on occasion.

TOURVEL: Why did she laugh?

VALMONT: I've no idea.

TOURVEL: Does she know about me?

VALMONT: No doubt she made what, in view of my past, must be regarded as a fair assumption.

(TOURVEL *seems almost convinced.*)

TOURVEL: I want to believe you.

VALMONT: I knew you were coming up, you were announced.

(*She looks at him, her eyes clear and candid.*)

TOURVEL: I'm sorry.

(VALMONT *flinches, a look of real guilt appearing. He takes her in his arms and she buries her face in his chest, weeping softly.*)

VALMONT: No, no, it's I who must apologize. It was most insensitive of me.

INT. VALMONT'S BEDROOM. DAY

TOURVEL *lies in* VALMONT's *arms. He looks down at her, profoundly contented.*

VALMONT: I didn't think it was possible for me to love you more, but your jealousy . . .

(*He breaks off, genuinely moved.* TOURVEL *looks up at him, speaks with the utmost simplicity.*)

TOURVEL: I love you so much.
(VALMONT *draws her up so that she's lying on top of him;
and kisses her, his expression uncharacteristically tender*.)
VALMONT: When will you start writing to me again?

EXT. COURTYARD OF VOLANGES'S HOUSE. NIGHT
VALMONT, *wrapped up against the blustery wind and wintry
rain, encounters the concierge in the courtyard. He hands over a
sum of money and the concierge admits him by a side door.*
MERTEUIL: (*Voice over*) 'My dear Vicomte: I don't believe
this self-denial can be good for you: I hope it doesn't
mean you're neglecting your little pupil.'

INT. CÉCILE'S BEDROOM. NIGHT
VALMONT *lies with* CÉCILE *in her large four-poster. They speak
in whispers.*
CÉCILE: But where can Danceny be?
VALMONT: I told you, I have all my people out looking: and
no trace of him.
(*The door suddenly bursts open.* CÉCILE *suppresses a shriek.*
VALMONT, *who is nearer the door, gets up after a few
seconds and tiptoes towards the gaping doorway. No one. He
closes the door with a sigh of relief and locks it.*)
Only the wind.
(*He turns back to discover that* CÉCILE *has vanished.*)
Where are you?
(*There's a groan from the far side of the bed. Hurrying over,*
VALMONT *discovers that* CÉCILE *has jammed herself in her
panic into the tiny space between the bed and the wall. He
helps her up, smiling: but* CÉCILE *looks anguished.*)
Nothing to worry about.
CÉCILE: Yes there is. I'm bleeding.

EXT. ENTRANCE AND COURTYARD OF MERTEUIL'S
HOUSE. NIGHT
The same windy and rainy night. MERTEUIL's *carriage turns in
at the entrance and comes to a stop in the courtyard. The porter
emerges from his lodge with a large open umbrella as footmen
converge on the carriage.*

Lurking in the archway which leads out to the street is AZOLAN.
*He moves so as to stay out of sight, peering into the courtyard to
try to identify the occupants of the carriage. After a while,
he reacts, with an expression of surprise and cynical
amusement.*

INT. CORRIDOR OF MIRRORS IN MERTEUIL'S HOUSE.
NIGHT
The house is deserted. VALMONT *moves stealthily down the
mirrored corridor, surrounded and apparently pursued by his
reflections. He stops and hesitates, looking from one mirror to
another. Then he remembers and applies pressure to one, opening
it to reveal the spiral staircase.*

INT. MERTEUIL'S BEDROOM. NIGHT
VALMONT *flicks back the curtains on Merteuil's four-poster to
reveal* MERTEUIL *and her new lover lying on the bed. For a
while the young man makes no move, hoping perhaps to escape
identification: vainly, since he is quite clearly* DANCENY.
MERTEUIL *has remained perfectly calm.*
VALMONT: Your porter seems to be under the impression you
   are still out of town.
MERTEUIL: I have in fact only just returned.
VALMONT: Without attracting the attention of your porter. I
   think it may be time to review your domestic
   arrangements.
MERTEUIL: I'm exhausted. Naturally I instructed the porter
   to inform casual callers that I was out.
   (VALMONT *checks a retort and turns instead, smiling, to*
   DANCENY.)
VALMONT: And you here as well, my dear young friend. The
   porter would seem to be having a somewhat erratic
   evening.
DANCENY: Oh, well, I, erm, yes.
VALMONT: As a matter of fact, it's you I'm looking for.
DANCENY: Is it?
VALMONT: Mademoiselle Cécile returns to Paris after an
   absence of over two months. What do you suppose is

uppermost in her mind? Answer, of course, the longed-for reunion with her beloved Chevalier.

MERTEUIL: Vicomte, this is no time to make mischief.

VALMONT: Nothing could be further from my mind, madame.

DANCENY: Go on.

VALMONT: Imagine her distress and alarm when her loved one is nowhere to be found. I've had to do more improvising than an Italian actor.

DANCENY: But how is she? Is she all right?

VALMONT: Oh, yes. Well, no, to be quite frank. I'm sorry to tell you she's been ill.

(DANCENY *is horrified.*)

DANCENY: Ill!

VALMONT: Calm yourself, my friend, the surgeon has declared her well on the road to recovery. But you can well imagine how desperate I've been to find you.

DANCENY: Of course, my God, how could I have been away at such a time? How can I ever forgive myself?

(*His voice trails away, as he becomes aware of* MERTEUIL*'s withering glance.*)

VALMONT: But, look, all is well now with Cécile, I assure you. And I shan't disturb you further.

(*He kisses* DANCENY *on both cheeks and then produces a piece of paper from an inside pocket.*)

It's only that I have something to show the Marquise.

(MERTEUIL *looks up sharply: he's succeeded in catching her interest. He shows her the letter. She reaches for it but he pulls it away again. She looks at him for a moment, amused.*)

MERTEUIL: Wait in my dressing-room. It's through there.

VALMONT: I know where it is.

(*He straightens up and begins to move away.*)

INT. MERTEUIL'S DRESSING-ROOM. NIGHT

MERTEUIL *finishes reading the letter. Its contents have obviously not pleased her, but she controls herself and looks up, her expression truculent.*

MERTEUIL: I see she writes as badly as she dresses.

(*Before* VALMONT *can respond, she changes the subject.*)
Is it really true the little one has been ill?
VALMONT: Not so much an illness, more a refurbishment.
MERTEUIL: What do you mean?
VALMONT: A miscarriage.
MERTEUIL: Oh, Vicomte, I am sorry. Your son and Bastide's heir.
VALMONT: Isn't there something else we should be discussing?
MERTEUIL: I do hope you're not going to be difficult about Danceny.
VALMONT: I know Belleroche was pretty limp, but I think you could have found a livelier replacement than that mawkish schoolboy.
MERTEUIL: Mawkish or not, he's completely devoted to me. And, I suspect, better equipped to provide me with happiness and pleasure than you. In your present mood.
VALMONT: I see.
(*He lapses into an injured silence. Then* MERTEUIL *smiles coquettishly.*)
MERTEUIL: If I thought you would be your old charming self, I might invite you to visit me one evening next week.
VALMONT: Really?
MERTEUIL: I still love you, you see, in spite of all your faults and my complaints.

INT. GRAND STAIRCASE. NIGHT
MERTEUIL *leads* VALMONT, *holding his hand. At the top of the grand staircase, he turns to her.*
VALMONT: Are you sure you're not going to impose some new condition before you agree to honour your obligation?
(*Pause.* MERTEUIL *considers how best to respond. Finally, she sets off down the stairs, speaking with deadly precision and calm.*)
MERTEUIL: I have a friend, who became involved with an entirely unsuitable woman. Whenever any of us pointed this out to him, he invariably made the same feeble reply:

it's beyond my control, he would say. He was on the verge
of becoming a laughing-stock. At which point, another
friend of mine, a woman, decided to speak to him
seriously. She explained to him that his name was in
danger of being ludicrously associated with this phrase for
the rest of his life. So do you know what he did?

VALMONT: I feel sure you're about to tell me.

MERTEUIL: He went round to see his mistress and bluntly
announced he was leaving her. As you might expect, she
protested vociferously. But to everything she said, to
every objection she made, he simply replied: 'it's beyond
my control.' Good night.

(*She turns and leaves him. For a while he doesn't move, but
stands deep in thought, his heart heavy.*)

INT. DRAWING-ROOM IN TOURVEL'S HOUSE. DAY
There's a fire burning in the grate. TOURVEL *paces anxiously up
and down. The door opens and* GEORGES *shows in* VALMONT.
*She runs across to him, unable to conceal her delight, and buries
herself in his arms. He embraces her, his expression strained and
weary. He sinks to his knees, still clasping her tightly.*

TOURVEL: You're only five minutes late, but I get so
frightened. I become convinced I'm never going to see
you again.

VALMONT: My angel.

TOURVEL: Is it like that for you?

VALMONT: Yes. At this moment, for example, I'm quite
convinced I'm never going to see you again.

(*He's still holding her close and she fails to discern the edge in
his voice. She laughs, still unconcerned.*)

TOURVEL: What?

(VALMONT *rises to his feet and breaks away from her. Now,
his expression is icy and* TOURVEL *feels an automatic stab of
fear.*)

VALMONT: I'm so bored, you see. It's beyond my control.

TOURVEL: What do you mean?

VALMONT: After all, it's been four months. So, what I say.
It's beyond my control.

TOURVEL: Do you mean . . . you don't love me any more?

VALMONT: My love had great difficulty outlasting your virtue. It's beyond my control.

TOURVEL: It's that woman, isn't it?

VALMONT: You're quite right, I have been deceiving you with Émilie. Among others. It's beyond my control.

TOURVEL: Why are you doing this?

(Until this point, every word has been dragged from VALMONT. Now, he turns on her to deliver the coup de grâce.)

VALMONT: There's a woman. Not Émilie, another woman. A woman I adore. And I'm afraid she's insisting I give you up. It's beyond my control.

(Suddenly TOURVEL rushes at him, fists flailing. They grapple silently and grimly for one moment, before she screams at him.)

TOURVEL: Liar! Liar!

VALMONT: You're right, I am a liar. It's like your fidelity, a fact of life, no more nor less irritating. Certainly, it's beyond my control.

TOURVEL: Stop it, don't keep saying that!

(He hurls her across the room; she crashes to the floor against the ottoman.)

VALMONT: Sorry. It's beyond my control.

(He closes his eyes and wills himself onwards.)

Why don't you take another lover?

(She bursts into tears, shaking her head and moaning incoherently.)

Whatever you like. It's beyond my control.

TOURVEL: Do you want to kill me?

(VALMONT strides over to her, takes her by the hair and jerks her head up.)

VALMONT: Listen. Listen to me. You've given me great pleasure. But I simply can't bring myself to regret leaving you. It's the way of the world. Quite beyond my control.

(He lets her go and she collapses full-length, moaning and sobbing helplessly. He hurries from the room. She remains where she is, utterly distraught.)

INT. ENTRANCE HALL. DAY
Outside the door VALMONT *has stopped. He can hear the sound of* TOURVEL's *weeping. He closes his eyes and leans his head back against the door for a moment, his expression tormented and queasy. His hand reaches for the doorknob, but he overcomes the temptation and hurries away.*

EXT. COURTYARD OF MERTEUIL'S HOUSE. NIGHT
VALMONT's *carriage clatters into the courtyard through swirling fog.* VALMONT *jumps down from the carriage and calls up to the* COACHMAN.
VALMONT: Tomorrow morning, early.
COACHMAN: My lord.
> (*He flicks his whip and the carriage moves off.* VALMONT *sets off towards the entrance, a black shape cutting through the fog.*)

INT. GRAND SALON IN MERTEUIL'S HOUSE. NIGHT
The two fires at either end of the great room reflect in the mirrored doors and sparkling chandeliers. Furniture has been drawn up round the fires, forming two islands of objects, leaving the centre of the room a bare arena. MERTEUIL, *alone in the room, sits at a small escritoire, writing.* VALMONT, *dishevelled, wigless, advances purposefully across the room, throwing his cloak to one side.* MERTEUIL *is unpleasantly surprised to see him, but overcomes her alarm.*
MERTEUIL: This is not your appointed night.
VALMONT: That story you told me, how did it end?
MERTEUIL: I'm not sure I know what you mean.
VALMONT: Well, once this friend of yours had taken the advice of his lady friend, did she take him back?
MERTEUIL: Am I to understand . . . ?
VALMONT: The day after our last meeting, I broke with Madame de Tourvel, on the grounds that it was beyond my control.
> (*A slow smile of great satisfaction spreads across* MERTEUIL's *face.*)
MERTEUIL: You didn't!

VALMONT: I certainly did.

MERTEUIL: But how wonderful of you.

VALMONT: You kept telling me my reputation was in danger, but I think this may well turn out to be my most famous exploit, I believe it sets a new standard. Only one thing could possibly bring me greater glory.

MERTEUIL: What's that?

VALMONT: To win her back.

MERTEUIL: You think you could?

VALMONT: I don't see why not.

MERTEUIL: I'll tell you why not: because when one woman strikes at the heart of another, she seldom misses; and the wound is invariably fatal.

VALMONT: Is that so?

MERTEUIL: Oh, yes; I'm also inclined to see this as one of my greatest triumphs.

VALMONT: There's nothing a woman enjoys as much as a victory over another woman.

MERTEUIL: Except, you see, Vicomte, my victory wasn't over her.

VALMONT: Of course it was. What do you mean?

MERTEUIL: It was over you.

(*Silence.* VALMONT*'s eyes are suddenly full of fear.* MER-TEUIL, *on the other hand, has never seemed more serene.*)
You loved that woman, Vicomte. What's more, you still do. Quite desperately. If you hadn't been so ashamed of it, how could you have treated her so viciously? You couldn't bear even the vague possibility of being laughed at. And this has proved something I've always suspected. That vanity and happiness are incompatible.

(VALMONT *is very shaken. He has to make an effort to be able to resume, his voice ragged with strain.*)

VALMONT: Whatever may or may not be the truth of these philosophical speculations, the fact remains it's now your turn to make a sacrifice.

MERTEUIL: Is that so?

VALMONT: Danceny must go.

MERTEUIL: Where?

VALMONT: I've been more than patient about this little whim of yours, but enough is enough.

MERTEUIL: One of the reasons I never remarried, despite a quite bewildering range of offers, was the determination never again to be ordered around. I must therefore ask you to adopt a less marital tone of voice.

VALMONT: She's ill, you know. I've made her ill. For your sake. So the least you can do is get rid of that colourless youth.

(*He slaps her face with his glove; but she simply looks back at him, brimming with confidence.*)

MERTEUIL: Haven't you had enough of bullying women for the time being?

(VALMONT's *face hardens.*)

VALMONT: I see I shall have to make myself very plain. I have come to spend the night. I shall not take at all kindly to being turned away.

MERTEUIL: I am sorry. I've made other arrangements.

(*A grim satisfaction begins to enliven* VALMONT's *features.*)

VALMONT: Yes. I knew there was something.

(MERTEUIL *sits, her expression icy.*)

MERTEUIL: What?

(VALMONT *settles himself opposite her, taking his time.*) What?

VALMONT: Danceny isn't coming. Not tonight.

MERTEUIL: What do you mean? How do you know?

VALMONT: I know because I've arranged for him to spend the night with Cécile.

(*Silence.* VALMONT *smiles.*)

Come to think of it, he did mention he was expected here. But when I put it to him that he really would have to make a choice, I must say he didn't hesitate. He's coming to see you tomorrow to explain; and to offer you, do I have this right, yes, I think I do, his eternal friendship. As you said, he's completely devoted to you.

(MERTEUIL *rises abruptly.*)

MERTEUIL: That's enough, Vicomte.

VALMONT: You're absolutely right.

(*He gets up, throwing his hat and gloves on to the sofa.*)
Shall we go up?

MERTEUIL: Shall we what?

(*VALMONT is taking off his coat, dropping it over the back of the sofa.*)

VALMONT: Go up. Unless you prefer this, if memory serves, rather purgatorial sofa.

MERTEUIL: I believe it's time you were leaving.

VALMONT: No. I don't think so. We made an arrangement. I really don't think I can allow myself to be taken advantage of a moment longer.

MERTEUIL: Remember I'm better at this than you are.

VALMONT: Perhaps. But it's always the best swimmers who drown. Now. Yes or no? Up to you, of course. I merely confine myself to remarking that a no will be regarded as a declaration of war. A single word is all that is required.

MERTEUIL: All right.

(*She looks at him evenly for a moment, until he concludes that she has made her answer and stretches out his hand to her. But he's wrong. The answer follows now, calm and authoritative.*)
War.

(*She leaves the room and VALMONT closes his eyes and lowers his head unhappily.*)

EXT. DRY MOAT. DAWN
There's snow on the ground: and the camera pans down towards the bare patch of earth under a bridge where VALMONT and DANCENY, épées in hand, circle one another in the grey dawn light. There are men in black on the bridge above; AZOLAN and the other seconds wait below. VALMONT bears down on DANCENY.

MERTEUIL: (*Voice over*) 'My dear Chevalier Danceny: I understand you spent last night with Cécile Volanges. I learnt this from her more regular lover; the Vicomte de Valmont.'

(*The duel begins, fierce and determined, VALMONT's skill against DANCENY's aggression. For a while they're evenly*

70

matched, with VALMONT, *clearly a talented swordsman,
looking the more dangerous. Very soon, he inflicts a small
wound under* DANCENY's *arm. Then he turns away
impatiently, throws aside his épée and takes another from the
case* AZOLAN *holds open. Then he advances menacingly on*
DANCENY, *who retreats, until, under the bridge,* VALMONT
*fells him and has him at his mercy. However, overcome by a
strange paralysis, he looks away.*)

INT. VALMONT'S BEDROOM. DAY
As before, VALMONT *draws up* TOURVEL, *so that she's lying
on top of him.*

EXT. DRY MOAT. DAWN
VALMONT *moves away, looking surprised at himself: and*
DANCENY *scrambles up.*

INT. PRIVATE ROOM IN THE CONVENT. DAY
The camera follows VOLANGES *and* CÉCILE *as, led by a nun,
their footsteps ring out on the stone flags of a high Gothic room.
They approach a curtained bed, where* TOURVEL *lies, deathly
pale. As they arrive at the bed,* TOURVEL *turns to look at*
VOLANGES.
TOURVEL: I'm dying because I wouldn't believe you.

EXT. DRY MOAT. DAWN
VALMONT *returns to the attack: they cut and parry with
immense energy. Then* VALMONT *skids in the snow and*
DANCENY, *more by luck than good judgement, succeeds in
wounding him in whichever is not his sword arm.* DANCENY
immediately withdraws, according to the rules. VALMONT
looks down at the wisp of blood staining his torn sleeve.

INT. TOURVEL'S ROOM IN THE CONVENT. DAY
TOURVEL *groans and struggles, held down by nuns, who heat and
apply cupping-bowls over the wounds produced in a cross-hatched
pattern by the surgeon's scarifier.*

EXT. DRY MOAT. DAWN
The duel continues: vicious thrust and parry, until VALMONT, *to* DANCENY's *surprise, suddenly turns his back on him and moves away.*

INT. VALMONT'S BEDROOM. DAY
As before, TOURVEL, *on top of* VALMONT, *kisses him passionately.*

EXT. DRY MOAT. DAY
VALMONT *turns back to* DANCENY *and the next pass degenerates into a brawl, which ends as* DANCENY *discovers* VALMONT's *blade at his throat. But, once again,* VALMONT *turns his back on* DANCENY.

INT. TOURVEL'S ROOM IN THE CONVENT. DAY
The surgeon's curved blade cuts at the vein on the inside of TOURVEL's *elbow and dark blood begins to flow into a small silver bowl.*

EXT. DRY MOAT. DAY
DANCENY *drives* VALMONT *back, but the effort brings him to his knees in the snow. Both are exhausted now and* DANCENY's *shirt is stained and mottled with the blood from numerous flesh wounds.* VALMONT *staggers away and leans against the cool stone wall rearing up from the moat.*
DANCENY *remains on his knees, gasping for breath.*
Close on VALMONT: *his hand slowly loosens its grip on the hilt of the épée until he's balancing it against the wall on one finger. He glances at* DANCENY *out of the corner of his eye. He lets his sword drop and at the same moment turns quickly away from the wall, running on to* DANCENY's *sword, which buries itself deep in his stomach. There's a moment of mutual shock and then* DANCENY *withdraws his blade.* VALMONT *slides down the wall, his face crashing into the snow.*
DANCENY *shouts to his second.*
DANCENY: Fetch the surgeon.
VALMONT: No, no.

DANCENY: Do as I say!

(*The second hurries away as* AZOLAN *drapes* VALMONT's *coat around him.* DANCENY *stands alone, uncertain.*)

VALMONT: A moment of your time.

(DANCENY *reluctantly approaches.*)

Two things: a word of advice, which of course you may ignore, but it is honestly intended; and a request.

DANCENY: Go on.

VALMONT: The advice is: be careful of the Marquise de Merteuil.

DANCENY: You must permit me to treat with scepticism anything you have to say about her.

VALMONT: Nevertheless, I must tell you: in this affair, we are both her creatures.

(*Painfully, he reaches into his coat pocket and brings out a bundle of letters.*)

As I believe her letters to me will prove.

(*He hands* DANCENY *the bloodstained package.*)

When you've read them, you may decide to circulate them.

DANCENY: And the request?

VALMONT: I want you somehow . . . somehow to get to see Madame de Tourvel . . .

DANCENY: I understand she's very ill.

VALMONT: That's why this is most important to me. I want you to tell her I can't explain why I broke with her as I did, but that since then my life has been worth nothing. I pushed the blade in deeper than you just have, my boy, and I need you to help me withdraw it. Tell her it's lucky for her that I've gone and I'm glad not to have to live without her. Tell her her love was the only real happiness I've ever known.

(*Close on* DANCENY: *tears are rolling down his cheeks.*)

Will you do that for me?

DANCENY: I will.

(DANCENY *raises a hand to brush away his tears.* AZOLAN *looks over at him indignantly.*)

AZOLAN: It's all very well feeling sorry now.

73

VALMONT: Let him be. He had good cause. I don't believe that's something anyone has ever been able to say about me. (*His head slumps to one side. He's dead. Overhead shot:* AZOLAN *and* DANCENY *kneel on either side of* VALMONT*'s body. All around, the snow is red with his blood.*)

INT. CONVENT. EVENING
DANCENY *strides through the cloisters.*

INT. TOURVEL'S ROOM IN THE CONVENT. EVENING
DANCENY *leans over* TOURVEL, *talking to her, unheard.*
VOLANGES *and* CÉCILE *wait in the background.*
TOURVEL *raises a hand and* DANCENY *stops speaking.*
TOURVEL: Enough.
   (*She looks up at* DANCENY.)
   Draw the curtains.
   (DANCENY *rises and draws the curtains on her bed. Behind the curtains,* TOURVEL *turns until her profile is silhouetted through the linen.*)

INT. TOURVEL'S ROOM IN THE CONVENT. NIGHT
The nuns close TOURVEL*'s eyes.*

INT. TOURVEL'S ROOM IN THE CONVENT. NIGHT
CÉCILE *stands by the deathbed as the nuns light the candles at the corners of the bed.*

INT. MERTEUIL'S DRESSING-ROOM. DAY
A great cry of anger and frustration; and then MERTEUIL *bursts into the room. She sweeps all her perfume boxes off the dressing-table. Then she smashes everything in the room she can possibly break, ornaments, mirrors, glass jars. Finally, she crashes to her knees, tearing at her clothes. A number of maids have arrived: they hover in the doorway appalled and she looks up at them, furious.*
MERTEUIL: Get out. Get out, all of you.
   (*They hurry away in something of a stampede.* MERTEUIL *kneels, desolate, in a field of glittering debris. Her head comes down again, contorted with misery and rage.*)

INT. MERTEUIL'S BOX AT THE OPERA. EVENING
It's before curtain-up and MERTEUIL *moves to the front of the
box to contemplate the house. Three boxes away a distinguished-
looking middle-aged couple are doing the same thing.* MERTEUIL
*bows to them. To her surprise, they turn away from her, ignoring
her ostentatiously. She turns to look down at the orchestra,
frowning; and becomes aware that the crowd below are murmuring
to one another and pointing up at her. Gradually, the hum dies
and there's silence in the theatre. Everyone in the stalls is looking
up at her. Suddenly, there's a hiss and then, growing quickly in
volume and intensity, a torrent of hissing and booing.* MERTEUIL
*absorbs it for a moment, then turns on her heel, her face an
impenetrable mask. She stumbles as she leaves the box.*

INT. MERTEUIL'S DRESSING-ROOM. NIGHT
Everything is back exactly as it was, leaving no trace of
MERTEUIL*'s rampage. She sits at her dressing-table, alone,
removing her make-up. As it comes off, a new* MERTEUIL *seems
for the first time to be revealed, weary, fragile, vulnerable almost.
She looks at her reflection with the anxiety someone feels in the
presence of their only friend: and the image slowly fades to black.*